GREATER NEW JERSEY

METROPOLITAN PORTRAITS

Metropolitan Portraits explores the contemporary metropolis in its

diverse blend of past and present. Each volume describes a North

American urban region in terms of historical experience, spatial

configuration, culture, and contemporary issues. Books in the

series are intended to promote discussion and understanding of

metropolitan North America at the start of the twenty-first century.

JUDITH A. MARTIN, SERIES EDITOR

GREATER

NEW JERSEY

Living in the Shadow of Gotham

DENNIS E. GALE

University of Pennsylvania Press | Philadelphia

10 9 8 7 6 5 4 3 2 1

Published by
University of Pennsylvania Press
Philadelphia, Pennsylvania 19104-4112

Library of Congress Cataloging-in-Publication Data

Gale, Dennis E.
    Greater New Jersey : living in the shadow of Gotham / Dennis E. Gale.
        p.   cm. — (Metropolitan portraits)
    Includes bibliographical references and index.
    ISBN-13: 978-0-8122-3954-6 (alk. paper)
    ISBN-10: 0-8122-3954-7 (alk. paper)
    1. New Jersey—Relations—New York (State)—New York.   2. New York
(N.Y.)—Relations—New Jersey.   3. New Jersey—History, Local.   4. City and town
life—New Jersey.   5. Regionalism—New Jersey.   6. Group identity—New Jersey.
7. New Jersey—Social conditions.   8. New York Region—Social conditions.
I. Title.   II. Series.
F134.G35   2006
974.9—dc22

                                                                    2006046156

To the victims and survivors
of the World Trade Center tragedy
of September 11, 2001

CONTENTS

FOREWORD
Judith A. Martin

Greater New Jersey: Living in the Shadow of Gotham is volume six of the expanding Metropolitan Portraits book series. In contemplating this series, the challenge of capturing *all* of the New York metropolitan area in one short book seemed insurmountable. I was thus delighted when Dennis Gale expressed his interest in writing about the Jersey-into-Manhattan stretch of this region. His idea struck me as eminently sensible: write about the lesser-known (except to its inhabitants) part of the region before taking on the better-known sections. Gale has done a masterful job of capturing the tone, challenges, and sensibilities of life across the river from "Gotham."

One might easily assume that, in the *Sopranos* era, we know more than ever about this broad trans-Hudson region. But such knowledge is partial and inevitably full of stereotypes. As Gale ably demonstrates, the roots of life in the North to South Jersey axis are indeed deeply historic: George Washington actually did sleep all over this region. But history here moved on quickly. The Hudson River cities on the Jersey side, from Elizabeth to Newark, rapidly became the industrial core of the region and prospered mightily in the nineteenth century, attracting legions of immigrants from southern and eastern Europe, as well as free blacks. From the 1960s, these same cities drew numerous new Hispanic residents, but still declined, as the pull of development passed them by. More recently, renewal and gentrification have refashioned certain of these cities, notably Hoboken and Jersey City, as the costs of living and working in Manhattan have escalated.

The intense and complex economic, social, and transit connections between the several Jersey subregions and Manhattan come alive here in all of their multiple variations. So does the inherent historical tension between the intense pull of Manhattan to the east and Philadelphia's weaker southerly influence. If this large Jersey region has had little independent identity over the decades, Gale helps readers understand why this is. As with every other North American metro area, the New York region massively spread out over the past five decades, creating landscapes of typical suburban subdivisions, business strips, and malls. Most visitors to New York—that is, to Manhattan—miss this. Thus they miss the essential character of this near-by Jersey multinodal axis.

Greater New Jersey highlights the complex and evolving regional relationships of recent decades. It reminds us that this was the first American metro area to think and plan regionally, beginning in the 1920s. Gale captures one fundamental New York/New Jersey reality in his lyrical description of "the karma of commuting"—into Manhattan but also out to suburban office and industrial parks. Short descriptions of the Manhattan communities most used by Jersey daytime commuters and evening entertainment-seekers yield to fuller explorations of communities from Paterson and Newark to Montclair and Morristown, the places where commuters actually live.

The "inside" culture of this broad Jersey axis is captured too. Corrupt politics and a certain tolerance of "goodfellas" may indeed be imbedded in some Jersey communities. Gale calls the Manhattan-North Jersey axis "a state of mind" rooted in place. This seems apt to any who first knew this region through its most famous musical sons, Sinatra and Springsteen. North Jersey may exist in a shadow, but it is one with its own imagination and cultural touchstones. Perhaps this slim volume will pique some to venture beyond the Hudson entertainment venues—Dennis Gale will prove an apt and well-informed guide.

PREFACE

The third millennium was just under way and the tyranny and
tragedy of September 11, 2001 was only months behind. And I
was a fledgling New Jerseyan, having arrived in the summer of
2000 to direct a new center for metropolitan studies on the Newark campus of Rutgers University. I was now a tiny fragment of
Greater New York, a colossus encompassing some 21 million people and 1,600 governments. I found myself challenged to embrace
the marvelous and bewildering complexity of a region clearly at a
significant turning point in its history. A new political regime occupied the nation's capital, the national economy was flagging,
and Americans worried about terrorist attacks. As a long-time student of American cities and regions, I realized that it was a propitious time to investigate my new home.

Happenstance and the annual meeting of the Urban Affairs Association in 2002 led me to Dr. Judith Martin and to the University
of Pennsylvania Press. Their newly conceived series, Metropolitan
Portraits, seemed the perfect vehicle from which to launch a
broadly conceived study of the region. Realizing that Greater New
York contains a larger population than every state except California, Judith and I agreed that my study might better center on a
smaller area, in this case what I term the "Manhattan-North Jersey
axis." By doing so I do not imply that, as goes the axis, so goes
Greater New York. I am quite confident nonetheless that similar
studies of Manhattan's relationships to the other New York boroughs, or to the New York or Connecticut suburbs, would yield

many similar insights. And yet, my research has been guided as much by these intraregional similarities as by what I suspect are unusual, if not unique, aspects of life in North Jersey which vary in degree, if not kind, from their counterparts in other U.S. metropolitan areas.

I am indebted to Dr. Judith Martin of the University of Minnesota for her support, insights, and editorial skills and to Robert Lockhart, history editor of the University of Pennsylvania Press, his able assistant, Laura Miller, and associate managing editor Erica Ginsburg. Their contributions are many and varied and I appreciate them. Exceeding my expectations, Judith, as series editor, went so far as to drive and walk the streets of Manhattan and North Jersey with me, the better to offer insights and raise questions. My case study on Hudson County was aided by Dr. Ellen Shoshkes, a consultant, author, and instructor, who guided me on my first visit to Hoboken and Jersey City in the fall of 2000. Neither she nor I imagined then that this study would ultimately come to fruition. Similarly, a guided tour of Newark in 2001 by my Rutgers colleague and friend Dr. Clement Price inspired me to write the case study on Essex County. He was ably assisted by Charles Cummings of the Newark Public Library, widely regarded as an authority on Newark and New Jersey history.

I am indebted to the Department of Public Administration and its chair, Dr. Marc Holzer, for support during the research and writing phases of this study. I thank my research assistant, Xu Hua, for his tireless talents in rooting out renegade monographs and preparing tables and charts. Several faculty colleagues at Rutgers served as informal sounding boards for the earlier phases of my research when, not infrequently, my observations were tentative and embryonic.

I am particularly indebted to Dr. Susan Fainstein of Columbia University and Dr. William Milczarski of Hunter College, both of whom participated in a panel on Greater New York that I organized at the 2002 Urban Affairs Association meetings; as long-term denizens of the region, they shared personal and professional observations and insights contributing much to the initial shaping of this volume, although they bear no responsibility for its final form. Happily, MIT faculty member Dr. Sam Bass Warner, Jr., author of the first volume in the series (on the Boston metropolis), appeared at that session. As one whose scholarship was seminal in nurturing my interests in urban history, Sam brought welcome encouragement to this project.

I am grateful for the rich scholarly resources made available to me by the combined libraries of Rutgers and especially by the Dana Library on the Newark campus. The propitious 2004 publication by Rutgers University Press of *The Encyclopedia of New Jersey*, edited by Maxine N. Lurie and Marc Mappen, was an unexpected blessing and it became a frequently consulted desk reference. In addition, I have drawn liberally on the poll archives of the Eagleton Institute of Politics at Rutgers, an invaluable resource for New Jerseyans. Finally, my research has benefited substantially from news coverage by area periodicals, especially the *Star-Ledger* and the *New York Times*. I am deeply indebted to many fine journalists whose contributions to public affairs reporting in Greater New York are immeasurable. I consider them fellow conspirators in the search for truth.

PROLOGUE

Into the Belly of the Beast

It is October 2, 2003 and my train departs at 4:20 p.m., leaving Morristown Station. We are bound for Manhattan. Morristown is west of Newark and New York City and my trip to Pennsylvania Station will take about an hour. If this were morning rush hour, jackets, suits, ties, and briefcases would abound as hundreds of commuters made their way to the canyons of Wall Street, Madison Avenue, and Midtown. But it is late afternoon now and gaggles of private school youths board, chattering in mobile sanctums, seemingly oblivious to those around them. Here and there I see darker faces, perhaps a Salvadoran housekeeper, a Jamaican child-care worker, or a Guatamalan landscaper. Three men wearing yarmulkes, students at a local rabbinical college, sit together. A woman leading a yellow Labrador retriever sits across from me, a trainer of seeing eye dogs at a local academy. A middle-aged couple walk down the aisle and seat themselves among college students, retired lawyers, off-duty police officers, and at least one university professor. They appear bound for a night at the opera or a Broadway show.

As we leave Morristown's center, our train will traverse similar communities such as Convent Station, Madison, Chatham, and Summit. Dating to the nineteenth century, our rail line has served for generations as a commuter corridor connecting affluent suburbanites to their jobs in Newark and Manhattan. Gazing through the window, I see patch after patch of oaks, maples, sycamores, and beeches. Backyards are shrouded in dogwood, Japanese maples, crab-apple trees, and forsythia, azalea, and rhododendron shrubs. The landscape here is a comfortable accordance between the seeming randomness of nature and the unmistakable purposefulness of landscapers and weekend gardeners. Cluster upon cluster of homes built in the mid-twentieth century punctuate the rolling hills. Colonials, split-levels, ranches, and Cape Cod cottages inscribe a landscape that for the most part remains wooded and green.

In the late nineteenth and early twentieth centuries this area became popular with the captains of industry. They erected great mansions on large estates and rode their horses over the rolling hills. Escaping New York, Newark, and other cities, they retreated westward to establish lavish compounds in communities with others like themselves. Over time, fortunes were depleted, descendants migrated, taxes climbed, and neighbors multiplied. Today, the brick, stone and wood-frame mansions of the early industrialists serve as college halls, lofty business addresses, and the headquarters of philanthropic institutions.

Passing through these affluent communities, I see pleasant, compact downtowns, their shops offering antiques, paintings, sculpture, women's clothing, shoes, books, furniture, hardware, and manicures. Above them are the professional offices of lawyers, doctors, investment brokers, psychotherapists, psychiatric social workers, family crisis counselors, and purveyors of holistic medicine, aromatherapy, Pilates, and yoga. Everywhere I look I am reminded that in these places the distinctions between human needs and human wants often blur, the fact being that for many households both are readily satisfied. I am also aware that history still lives out here, as evidenced by the area's many carefully preserved period buildings, parks, and monuments. Yet, none of these towns appears particularly pretentious. It seems as though people who reside in this area have made a statement, both about crowded, dangerous cities to the east and sprawling, boring subdivisions to the west. Still, I can't help noticing at every station that nineteenth century ambience is interrupted by twentieth-century technology, as row upon row of parked autos, SUVs, and minivans provide the glue holding life and livelihood together.

Our train enters Short Hills, one of the most exclusive addresses in New Jersey. I am reminded that at about this time three days earlier, a fifty-three-year-old unemployed former Wall Street investment banker knelt down on the tracks as a train approached. After the suicide, the police found the man's seven-year-old son lifeless in his bedroom. The boy's mother was at work in Manhattan. The family was facing mortgage foreclosure on their half-million-dollar home and debts totaling about $60,000. How, I wonder, can things go so terribly wrong in the midst of such wealth and privilege? But the remainder of the trip will only reinforce the contrasts between privilege and success, on the one hand, and struggle and deprivation, on the other.

My train soon approaches the adjoining towns of Maplewood and South Orange and I enter a different zone. Although these towns appear much like those behind us, their most compelling difference is not apparent to the eye. These towns abound with younger middle- and upper-middle-class families, the breadwinners of which work in Manhattan or in North and Central Jersey. Their town centers are smaller and somewhat less precious than those behind us; yet a house priced under $350,000 is rare. What distinguishes Maplewood and South Orange is race. Once these towns were peopled largely by Jewish American, Irish American, and Italian American families. Today, religion and ethnicity are not as prominent identifiers, and race, education, and sexual orientation have become more compelling features. Fearing white flight, a biracial citizen's coalition here has mobilized for more than a decade to discourage block-busting and to build racial trust. But here and in a few other North Jersey towns many people have found that living in an interracial community does not necessarily breed social cohesion. Racial friction in Maplewood or South Orange appears to be uncommon, yet people tend to socialize along racial lines.

In 2000 the towns' populations were each approximately one-third African American. Yet, Maplewood's black families are concentrated on the east side of town, nearer Newark, where properties are less costly. Whites are more prevalent in the more expensive areas of town, to the center and the western side. White families tend to patronize stores in downtown Maplewood, while African Americans are more likely to shop in downtown South Orange. And though both whites and nonwhites suffer during economic downturns, there is a nagging uneasiness that blacks often have a narrower margin of financial security than whites. Meanwhile, adding to Maplewood's liberal identity is the growing number of rainbow-patterned flags flying on front porches, as gay and lesbian couples with children settle into the community. It is in towns such as these that some of the loftiest tenets of the egalitarian society are being put to the test.

Within minutes of our train's departure from South Orange, the landscape changes abruptly. We have entered Orange, and ahead lie East Orange and Newark. Now, only African Americans climb aboard and virtually no whites deboard. These communities make up another zone, one composed of too much poverty, crime, and disrepair. The gentle hand of nature, only a few miles behind us, has succumbed to the harsh tyranny of asphalt, concrete, and aging brick. The faded emblems of once-thriving communities— churches, synagogues, libraries, city halls, and banks—still stand. In these towns, territory is defined not by stockade and picket fencing but instead by rusting chain link and corkscrews of glistening razor wire. Seedy apartment buildings are crammed cheek-by-jowl with faded frame houses. Most owners struggle to keep their homes up but are challenged by adjacent houses with blackened windows and scattered debris.

When the sun is at just the right angle, broken glass and discarded metal glitter on broken pavement and grassless lots. Junkyards whiz by, stacked with the compressed remains of yesterday's automobiles. Scattered here and there are small office buildings with large signs imploring passersby to lease vacant space. Several stores cast blank stares to the street, their interiors shielded from view by ubiquitous metal shutters. Knots of unemployed young men appear at corners, abandoned storefronts, and bus shelters. Discarded drink and fast-food containers litter sidewalks, gutters, and yards. On nearly every vertical surface are murals of polychromatic graffiti in flowing or geometric shapes; for the unpracticed eye, many are indecipherable. Are they put there by gangs marking turf? Perhaps they are simply the silent voices of dispirited youths declaring, "I exist!"

In spite of their problems, these mean streets are more positive than they appear to be. Life and activity abound in towns such as Orange, East Orange, and Newark. Greetings come easily to people on the streets, and smiles challenge the grimness of their surroundings. On almost every block a small drama is played out in laughter, gesturing hands, and rolling eyes, as the sheer spirit of human dignity pushes back the gloom in a theater where, for many, hope is a bit player. Unrecognizable through the windows of a passing train is the fact that these communities harbor small armies of everyday heroes and heroines who carry on their selfless efforts through public, religious, and charitable work.

No matter how many times I make this trip, I marvel at the contrasts separating what lies before me and what lies behind. Only a short while ago I gazed at places where little seems left to chance, where nearly everyone is able to exert their will on their own surroundings. Here, however, the tables are turned. To live in poor communities is to be surrounded by the unpredictable, the unexplainable, the inescapable. In affluent settings, death at one's own hand can come from expecting too much from life. Here, death is more likely to come at the hands of those who expect very little.

We leave Newark's classical revival train station and continue east. Below I see the city's ancient Broad Street, once thronging with streetcars, pedestrians, shoppers, and bustling stores. Now it is little more than a multi-lane highway delivering suburban workers to and from their downtown jobs. In the distance I see the historic Washington and Military parks, standing today as reminders of the New England-style commons they once were. Struggling street-level shops in many aging buildings are surmounted by upper floors with unlit windows. Here and there a glimmer of optimism is revealed in a renovated older office building, generating desperately needed tax revenues for city hall.

In the midst of it all, the city's handsome performing arts center appears. Iconic and prideful, it is evidence to many that Newark's much-vaunted renaissance has begun. Nearby, a minor league baseball park struggles to draw crowds and pay its bills. Here and there, beautiful church spires and domes puncture the skyline and once-proud commercial buildings await rescue. Civic, business, educational, and religious organizations keep the faith and labor year after year to move the city forward.

My train continues east across the dark, lifeless Passaic River. Like Newark, the adjacent towns were once enclaves of grinding, hissing, clanging industrial might. Today they house the hollow remains of mills, factories, and warehouses. At one time the river's shore was lined with companies producing plastics, paints, coal gas, petroleum, alkali, electrical apparatus, and assorted chemicals. In their wake, begrimed by decades of industrial smoke, are gas tanks, railroad sidings, junction boxes, concrete silos, electrical transformers, wooden crates, and a gaggle of overhead wires. Even the soil is a poultice of soot, cinder, and ash. Piles of industrial *shmuts* appear in scattered profusion. Soon we pass from wasteland to wetland. The Jersey Meadowlands, once a pristine gateway to Manhattan, later became a sprawling dumping ground for islands of warehouses, parking lots, mounds of discarded tires, scrap metal salvage yards, and stacks of concrete railroad ties. Thanks to a generous supply of mobsters, even human remains have been dumped here. For example, on a summer evening in 1929 one Eugene Moran, a hapless foot soldier for the Manhattan gangster Arnold Rothstein, was dispatched with a bullet to the head, his body then consumed in an incinerated Packard.[1] The most notorious resident *post mortem*, though, may be the late labor leader Jimmy Hoffa, whose body is rumored to occupy a final resting ground somewhere in the Meadowlands.[2] Though it is likely that human remains can be found, there is no doubt that the remains of human activity are everywhere. New Jersey Transit and PATH rolling stock are stored here. Somewhere, the granite columns of New York's magnificent classical revival Pennsylvania Station, demolished in the 1960s in the name of progress, lie interred.[3] Factories with corporate names such as Sherman Williams, Benjamin Moore, Ashland, Getty, Monsanto, and Diamond Alkali once prospered in this hapless landscape. They churned out everything from automobiles, mothballs, paint, playing card lacquer, creosote, and petroleum products to talcum powder, gypsum wallboard, coal gas, chromium, and mercury.[4]

On the north side of the train I spy I-280, its lanes filling with Manhattan workers returning home to a hundred North Jersey communities. We cross under the New Jersey Turnpike, now more than half a century old. Reminiscent of a Roman aqueduct, its towering piers and concrete roadbed curve serpent-like into the distance. To the south lies an engineering landmark, the Pulaski Skyway, its steel span connecting Newark, Jersey City, the Holland Tunnel, and Manhattan over the course of more than three miles. Opened in 1932, it appears like an ordinary steel bridge stretched to an extraordinary length as it surmounts a sea of cattails and legions of muskrats below.

My train crosses the Hackensack River. Immediately to the north rises an unlikely mound of igneous rock, informally known as Little Snake Hill, on which once resided billboards advertising Bromo-Seltzer and Coca-Cola. A park is planned for the site but years ago its environs were a favored depository for such unwanted facilities as a penitentiary, an almshouse, and hospitals for the mentally ill and elderly.[5] Farther east we pass by inky lagoons ringed by carpets of *Phragmites communis,* a tasseled reed that serves as North Jersey's "amber waves of grain."[6] Here and there, the murky waters are disturbed by a discarded truck body or a cluster of castoff rubber tires. As usual, my eyes search for my friend the great egret. The bird stakes out this terrain for daily foraging, its snowy feathers a declaration against the colorless backcloth of marshland. Today, I'm in luck. The egret is at work and I take small comfort that, for one more day at least, this waterfowl has held forth against foul waters. I watch his image fade and I wonder, is he really a sole proprietor of these marshes or does he have accomplices?

Soon we are passing countless tractor trailers and delivery trucks parked in regimental formations on acres of asphalt pads. A testament to the subregion's limitless appetite for consumer goods, they stand poised to feed the insatiable maw that is Greater New York. Outside my window I see a range of trash mounds that contour the otherwise flat landscape. Now swaddled in grass and young trees, these topographical anomalies shroud millions of tons of coffee grounds, egg shells, tin cans, orange peels, chicken bones, black plastic trash bags, newspapers, fractured fridges, and remaindered ranges. Like factories, each mound produces methane gas and vile streams of leachate, as bacteria slowly decompose their contents into the wetlands.[7] Decades ago, these man-made summits burned continuously, churning out an obscurant smudge across the blue sky, a testament to the low regard in which the region's citizens once held the Meadowlands.

Although dumping has largely ceased, the Meadowlands' servitude to the ravages of instant obsolescence has not. In the distance I spy a state-of-the-art incinerator plant, its high-tech stacks exhaling an almost imperceptible plume of white smoke. Once, I muse, smoke stacks were all about producing things in North Jersey. Today, they are more likely to be about disposing of things made anywhere in the world.

For a moment the train's lights flicker out as the engine shifts from diesel to electric power, a signal that we are about to enter the tubes under the Hudson River. To my right I see the Hoboken and Jersey City skylines, a curious blend of industrial decay and postmodern rebirth. Then we plunge through the basaltic palisades, pass under Union City and Weehawken, and angle downward below the Hudson River. Above our heads flow river barges, tugs, pleasure craft, polychlorinated biphenyls, even *striped bass!* I wonder if any fellow passengers this day share the nightmare that has haunted me ever since September 11, 2001: a terrorist's bomb explodes, there are screams, fire, and smoke, then darkness as millions of gallons of river water rush into the train. For distraction, I remind myself that a century ago it was impossible for people to pass *under the river* and that yesterday's technological marvel has become today's ho-hum event.

In a few minutes our train arrives at Penn Station. We pour onto the platform, climb the comatose escalator, and enter the main concourse. It is now rush hour and the homeward-bound hordes are milling about, shoulder to shoulder, awaiting their trains. I adopt the appropriate thousand-yard stare and propel myself through their numbers. I make my way to the men's room and am reminded of my favorite irony about Penn Station. Several years ago authorities began piping symphonies and concertos into the concourse. Studies had shown that crime, vandalism and vagrancy decreased when potential perpetrators were serenaded with the likes of Mozart, Hayden, and Brahms. (More modern composers go unplayed, prompting my suspicion that the likes of Debussy, Shostakovich, and Graffe bring out the worst in pickpockets and flashers). Awaiting my turn in the odoriferous rest room, I marvel at how supremely disjunctive it is to be answering nature's call to the strains of Hayden's Trumpet Concerto in E-flat Major, while standing elbow-to-elbow with street people and perhaps an ad executive, a private detective, a heating and air conditioning mechanic, and a defrocked clergyman.

I continue on my way to the subway station, round a corner and am confronted by a freshet of anxious commuters. The turnstiles act as sluice gates and I dodge to the right and hug the tiled wall as the torrent rushes by. Some eyes appear panicked, a testament to the threat of a missed train home. I feel like a spawning salmon swimming upstream and hope that I'm not about to be swept away. Once on the subway, I stand immobile, ever intent on respecting the personal space of those around me. It is nearly 6 p.m., the cars are full, riders are remarkably civilized, and in fifteen minutes I will be at my destination.

In little more than an hour my trip has taken me from the periphery to the center of one of the most phenomenal metropolitan regions anywhere in the world. Once again I have collected a core sample to add to a storehouse of memories. I wonder, will this trip ever become mundane?

I hope the foregoing will leave the reader with some sense of the fascination I have found in living in Greater New York. In the following chapters I have tried to craft a richer portrait of this subregion, centering on the theme of "divided dominion." While tensions and cleavages between central cities and their suburbs are common throughout metropolitan America, I argue that the historical and contemporary relationships between Manhattan and North Jersey present a special case. As part of the most heavily populated central city and metropolitan region in North America, North Jersey has been vastly overshadowed by the global stature of New York City. And even though New Jersey has made important strides in redressing economic, political, and cultural imbalances, the dominance of Manhattan's organizations and institutions has contributed to an odd struggle within North Jersey over image, identity, and social cohesiveness. Moreover, North Jersey's historic progress in accommodating a huge variety of racial, ethnic, religious, and cultural groups is now occurring in a landscape of severely declining space and resources. State and local government responses to growth over many decades have further confounded any sense of sub-regional identity and coherence. Among the issues I discuss are the management of trans-Hudson conflicts, the stresses of enormous population density and diversity, the impacts of growth and development, and the miniaturization of local government. Also examined are the corrosive effects on North Jersey identity of the New York-based mass media and professional sports industries and the detrimental influences on civic pride and trust posed by organized crime and official misconduct.

CHAPTER ONE

The Bi-State Brokerage of Power

Endless books, articles, and films have familiarized people across the United States and around the globe with New York City. It is quite possibly the most recognizable city on Earth. Perhaps more than a billion people have some perception of Gotham. In truth, however, it is the borough of Manhattan, the heart of Greater New York, with which most of them are familiar. New York's other boroughs—Brooklyn, Queens, the Bronx, and Staten Island— although very much a part of this great city, share a considerably less exalted identity. Across the Hudson River, North Jersey's nearest counties, like the four boroughs, are first-tier Manhattan suburbs. Encircling these inner-ring communities are the New York State, Connecticut, and New Jersey outer tier counties (Map 1, p. 14). This study centers on Manhattan and the North Jersey counties, which I term the "Manhattan-North Jersey Axis" of Greater New York. Further on I will distinguish between the inner- and outer-tier North Jersey counties.

The state of New Jersey is small by national standards. Ranked forty-sixth in land area among the fifty states, it is a fraction of the size of its larger neighbors, New York State and Pennsylvania. Yet, New Jersey's population in 2000 (more than 8.4 million) ranked ninth-largest among states nationally.[1] As the most densely populated of the fifty states, New Jersey lies almost completely within

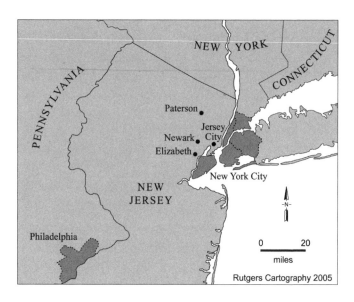

Map 1. Greater New York encompasses parts of New York State, Connecticut, and New Jersey. North Jersey, lying between New York City and Philadelphia (darker shading), includes Newark, Jersey City, Paterson, and Elizabeth.

the combined New York and Philadelphia metropolitan areas. Squeezed between its larger neighbors, the state appears on a map to be an after thought, its improbable wiggle-waggle shape lending a tentative, indecisive appearance.[2] But in fact the Garden State is in a highly strategic location and its myriad transportation corridors funnel millions of people and products through the northeastern United States annually. One dimension of this flow is the daily flood of Manhattan-North Jersey commuters.

A HIGHLY PERMEABLE BORDER

Every weekday tens of thousands of workers cross the Hudson, the vast majority headed to Wall Street or Midtown, Times Square or other corporate enclaves. Though some New Jerseyans work on Staten Island or in the other boroughs, perhaps three hundred thousand or more of them commute daily to Manhattan.[3] But suburbanization over the past thirty years, aided by new highways and rail and intercity bus services, has expanded the New York "commutershed" to the more distant counties of North and Central Jersey and eastern Pennsylvania. Some commuters drive or take a bus across the George Washington Bridge or through the Lincoln or Holland tunnels (Map 2, p. 22). Others take the New Jersey Transit or PATH trains under the Hudson River. Smaller numbers take the ferries departing from several ports on the North Jersey side of the river. The vast majority work in executive or professional positions in financial services, insurance, real estate, health, law, advertising, the performing arts, education, communications, fashion, or government. Others work in basic services, taking jobs, for example, as retail clerks, apartment and hotel doormen, security guards, or operators of taxi cabs, trucks, vans, limousines, buses, trains, or subways.

On weeknights, weekends, and holidays, the commuters are supplanted by tourists, many of whom also come from North and Central New Jersey. Thousands of teenagers and twenty-somethings are drawn to the bright lights of Times Square or trendy enclaves such as the Upper East Side, the Lower East Side, and SoHo. School groups and families with young children troop to the Empire State Building, South Street Seaport, Madison Square Garden, the Intrepid aircraft carrier, or the tour boat docks from which they depart for the Statue of Liberty, Ellis Island, or other sites. Some people visit Manhattan's many cultural attractions, such as museums, galleries and the theater. Many Jerseyans come simply to hang out, visit friends or lovers, patronize countless Manhattan eateries, or people watch. In this regard, they are little different from their suburban New York, Long Island, or Connecticut counterparts.

Although considerably smaller than the Jersey-to-Manhattan flows, the Manhattan-to-Jersey traffic has grown, especially over the past two decades. But Manhattanites seem to travel to North Jersey primarily for employment, especially in advanced services such as biotechnology, higher education, finance, and insurance. Even so, North Jersey communities have drawn home seekers from Manhattan for generations. Over the past three decades, for example, a flood of young adults from Manhattan and the gentrified neighborhoods of Brooklyn have relocated to the lofts and apartments of Hoboken and Jersey City. Gay and straight couples have migrated to the older middle- and upper-income suburbs of North Jersey such as Englewood, Ridgefield, Montclair, Glen Ridge, Maplewood, South Orange, West Orange, and Westfield. Seeking homes with more space and towns with better schools and security, they seem little different from suburban-bound city dwellers elsewhere in North America. Many maintain their jobs in Manhattan and become North Jersey commuters. Old allegiances die hard however, and many ex-Gothamites retain a kind of dual citizenship: in their heads they are Jerseyans but in their hearts they are expatriate New Yorkers.

Yet, the quest for a happy home drives North Jerseyans to Manhattan, too. Two, three, four, or more young adults cram themselves into apartments in youth ghettoes on the Upper East Side, the Lower East Side, Greenwich Village, or the East Village or near institutions such as Columbia University. Empty-nesters flee suburban home maintenance and long job commutes when their children are independent, settling in the myriad cooperative and condominium towers of the Upper West Side, Midtown, and Battery Park City. Workers and retirees alike, they invest their newfound leisure time in Manhattan's inexhaustible supply of gustatory, entertainment and cultural attractions.

GREATER NEW YORK AND THE EASTERN MEGALOPOLIS

As Jean Gottmann pointed out more than forty years ago, Greater New York is in large measure the crossroads of the urbanized northeast. At the time, this megalopolis stretched from southern New Hampshire to the Chesapeake Bay and encompassed parts of nine states, including all of New Jersey.⁴ Today it stretches even farther to the north, south, and west. And Greater New York persists as its center of population, economic activity and culture. But the New York metropolitan region has become much more intimately connected to the global economy by worldwide immigration flows, information technology and trade. Thus, though Greater New York remains physically in and of the eastern megalopolis, it is linked in innumerable interdependent ways to global capitals such as Hong Kong, Singapore, Taiwan, Seoul, London, Paris, Toronto, and Rio de Janeiro.⁵

Although megalopolitan and global influences are critical to understanding Greater New York, the metropolitan region itself is a forbidding challenge for serious study. If the tri-state region composing Greater New York became a single state with its own government, its 2000 population of more than 21 million would exceed that of Texas, currently the second most populated state after California. Adding to its bewildering character, however, is Greater New York's enormous population density and diversity, its elaborate web of transportation corridors, and the fact that governance is spread across three states and more than 1,600 local government units. Though similarities exist in other North American metropolises such as Toronto, Mexico City, Chicago, and Los Angeles, it is doubtful that any contend with the sheer complexity of political, economic, and social conditions found in Greater New York.

Like Nassau and Westchester counties in New York State, North Jersey shares a border with New York City. The Hudson River, a slender ribbon of water, places the Garden State cheek-by-jowl with its neighbor. Consequently, North Jerseyans are faced with more frequent bi-state challenges than southern Connecticut residents; sometimes political interaction, if not federal intervention, is required. While the balance of regional political and economic power continues to reside in New York City, growth and development in New Jersey over the past thirty years has somewhat diminished the state's dependence on the city's employment, income, and business opportunities. In part owing to these forces, the negotiation of bi-state contention in recent years has proceeded on terms more often friendly to the interests of North Jerseyans. Later in this chapter I will discuss some examples.

Not all, perhaps not even most, of New York City's prime influences on North Jersey life are rooted in government actions. In subsequent chapters I offer three examples, each of which helps to shape the culture of North Jersey life. These are local news dissemination, professional sports, and organized crime. Other factors arise from within the state itself. North Jersey's enormous population density and social diversity, diminishing reserves of land and resources, and fragmented local government structure, for example, are issues I probe. These dimensions, I argue, challenge the subregion's limits of environmental sustainability and social cohesion even as they underscore New Jerseyans' impressive capacity to accommodate extraordinary difference within extremely tight constraints of space. Nonetheless, I conclude that North Jersey cannot be understood apart from its intricate network of relationships with New York City. Although proximity has brought many opportunities to North Jerseyans, it has also contributed to the challenges of internal identity.

THE EMERGENCE OF BI-STATE CONFLICT

It would be easy to conclude that conflict between North Jersey and Manhattan is a product of new transportation innovations put in place in the early twentieth century. Indeed, the automobile and bridge and tunnel construction did much to enhance intercourse across the Hudson River. In fact, however, tensions along the Manhattan-North Jersey axis can be traced to the seventeenth century. And even after the British took control of New Amsterdam, renaming it New York, conflict continued. At the time, today's New Jersey was divided into two provinces, East and West Jersey. New York denied customs status to East Jersey's port city, Perth Amboy, thereby preventing the unloading of international cargo on the Jersey shore.[6] Added to these tensions were royal threats to annex the province of East Jersey (roughly corresponding to today's North Jersey) to New York. In 1702 the British crown relocated the seat of government over the Jerseys to New York and the two provinces were thereafter governed as a single colony called New Jersey. But the first royal governor, Lord Edward Cornbury, who sometimes appeared in public dressed in women's clothing, wig and makeup, did little to inspire faith among Jerseyans regarding his leadership qualities.[7] Later, New York claimed dominion over Staten Island, overlooking the fact that it is a few hundred yards from the Jersey shoreline and more than two miles from New York. During the Revolutionary War, New York was occupied by the British and New Jersey became a convenient battleground.[8] For a time New Jersey was occupied by English troops, as General George Washington's continental soldiers and militia engaged the enemy in several battles and skirmishes.

Independence and statehood brought New Jerseyans a measure of political sovereignty. But New York maintained economic supremacy. For example, New York merchants often failed to accept currency issued by the state of New Jersey. Furthermore, ships arriving at or departing from New Jersey piers by way of New York City were subject to entrance and clearance fees. Conflict across the Hudson was inflamed yet again over the post-Revolutionary War debate leading up to the Great Compromise.[9] Once more, however, New York asserted its supremacy when in 1789 the young Congress chose to locate the seat of the new U.S. government temporarily in New York.[10]

Trans-Hudson mistrust continued into the nineteenth century.

One of the landmark legal cases in American jurisprudence grew out of a series of actions taken by the New York legislature from 1809 to 1811. These measures gave Robert Fulton and a partner a monopoly over steamboat ferry service between North Jersey and New York. In retaliation, the New Jersey legislature gave Colonel Aaron Ogden a similar monopoly between the two states. In 1824 the U.S. Supreme Court ruled in *Gibbons v. Ogden* that the federal government, not the states, had authority to regulate interstate commerce.[11] Both states were free to charter ferry service. Thus, the basis for bi-state conflict was negotiated not by the states themselves but by a federal intermediary. This would not be the last time that the two states would have to turn to higher authority to settle disputes.

With the opening of rail service in the nineteenth century, North Jersey became a critical transportation corridor for passengers and goods traveling to Manhattan, Philadelphia, and points beyond. Businessmen and public officials in both states found it in their interests to keep passengers and goods moving with as few disruptions as possible. A growing web of business ties brought greater momentum for bi-state cooperation.[12] New York bankers and lawyers, for example, handled the complicated affairs of businessmen and land owners in North Jersey's prosperous agricultural, mining and shipping communities. New York investors purchased North Jersey property or acquired shares in new business ventures there. For example, in 1804 a partnership headed by Alexander Hamilton to establish a port city in North Jersey received monopoly authority over land and governance from the New Jersey legislature. Although Hamilton's death stalled the venture, Jersey City would eventually rise on the site to become the state's primary shipping port.[13] Thus, even in the face of periodic and monumental bi-state conflicts, economic cooperation for mutually rewarding ventures played a critical role in relationships between Manhattan and North Jersey.

THE PORT AUTHORITY AND THE BI-STATE BROKERAGE OF POWER

By the beginning of the twentieth century, the New York and North Jersey ports were among the busiest in the nation. Leaders in both states recognized that better coordination and cooperation was necessary. In 1921 the Port of New York Authority was established by both state legislatures and the U.S. Congress. The Authority was given power over port activities within a large zone encompassing the five boroughs of New York City, as well as Newark, Jersey City, and several other North Jersey communities.[14] Even though its powers were limited during its infancy, the Authority became a forum for discourse, permitting both states to air political and economic issues of mutual concern. Authority leaders quickly established an identity as politically neutral experts in technical fields such as civil engineering, planning, and finance. Such attributes ensured that the Authority would become the primary engine for economic development in Greater New York. However, the Authority continues to struggle with stubborn self-interest on both sides of the Hudson from parochial politicians, entrenched railroad owners, and others.[15] Furthermore, because it is headquartered in Manhattan, the organization contends with allegations that its board and staff tilt toward New York in their priorities.

In more than eighty years of existence the Port Authority has significantly advanced transportation opportunities and economic development between North Jersey and New York City. Though the Hudson was breached in 1908 by two underground railroad tubes between North Jersey and Manhattan, automobile travel was possible only by ferry.[16] In the late 1920s and early 1930s the Authority built three spans, the Bayonne Bridge in Hudson County, the Goethals Bridge in Union County, and the Outerbridge Crossing in Middlesex County, all linking North Jersey to Staten Island.[17]

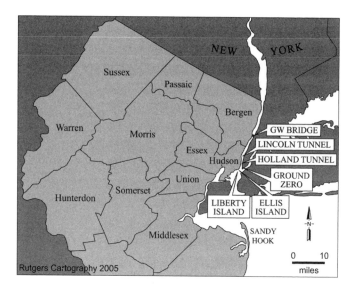

Map 2. Bergen, Essex, Hudson, Passaic, and Union counties make up Inner North Jersey, the state's primary area of growth during most of the twentieth century. The remaining counties, or Outer North Jersey, grew most rapidly after 1970.

The first vehicular link between Manhattan and North Jersey however, was the Holland Tunnel, which opened in 1927 (Map 2). It was built by a temporary bi-state agency and ownership was transferred to the Authority in 1931.[18] Perhaps the Authority's signature project during its infancy was the George Washington Bridge, which opened in 1931 and linked Fort Lee, New Jersey to North Manhattan.[19] Midtown Manhattan and Weehawken, New Jersey were connected when the Lincoln Tunnel opened in 1938.[20] With the proliferation of automobile ownership after World War I, these new corridors interwove New York City and North Jersey in ways that would forever change the intensity of their relationship and their mutual fortunes.[21] Whatever surface impressions people had at the time, the underlying reality was that Manhattan and North Jersey could not get along without each other. Thus, as the Great Depression and the New Deal unfolded, the mighty Hudson no longer demarcated a physical barrier to commerce and human intercourse. Increasingly, it was regarded as a scenic feature, albeit with vague and mischievous geopolitical implications. Through the bi-state brokerage of power, the barrier had been penetrated and the futures of the two polities were further intertwined.

After World War II, the Authority continued to expand its power as the chief builder and operator of transportation and economic development projects serving bi-state interests. For example, additional underwater tubes were added to the Lincoln Tunnel in 1945 and 1952.[22] In 1947 the agency assumed operation of the region's three major airports and Newark's seaport, greatly expanding air and shipping capacity and efficiency.[23] The Port Authority Bus Terminal, which opened in midtown Manhattan in 1950, improved Manhattan-North Jersey mass transit linkages.[24] By mid-century, Manhattan and North Jersey were joined—if not at the heart or the head—at the hip.

Throughout the 1960s and 1970s, however, the Authority's responsibilities began to shift. The postwar years had seen substantial suburban growth in North Jersey, which increased commuting to New York. Many commuters were baby-boomers who had left Manhattan because of crime, deteriorating conditions, and the high costs of housing; now they were raising their families in North Jersey's suburbs. Not only was the Garden State attracting population away from Gotham, it was making commuting to Manhattan easier for suburbanites. From the 1950s to the 1970s the state opened several super highways linking North Jersey to regional and national markets and suppliers in all directions (Map 4, p. 52). These corridors enabled businesses to locate near North Jersey interchanges and enjoy easy access to New York while avoiding the high costs and inconveniences of maintaining a New York address. Particularly in the late 1960s and throughout the 1970s, many corporations left Manhattan for Southern Connecticut, suburban New York and North Jersey in response to the city's fiscal crisis, concerns about crime and safety, and rising costs of office space and taxes.[25] Thus, North Jersey expanded its identity as a collection of bedroom suburbs and a source of skilled workers for New York, as well as a transportation corridor and a location for office expansion. Many in Manhattan's business and political communities felt threatened by these trends. Not perhaps coincidentally, the Authority remained firmly slanted toward New York's economic dominance, finding itself under pressure to help the city reverse its flagging fortunes. It was in this climate that the Authority announced plans in the early 1960s to build what would become the World Trade Center.

Until this time, the Authority was identified with regional transportation and economic development. Few observers considered the building of office towers a part of the agency's portfolio. Moreover, proposing to construct not one, but two, of the tallest office towers in the world was criticized as brazen and ill-advised. As plans crystallized, opposition from New Jersey politicians surfaced. After considerable debate, the project survived through a negotiated quid pro quo requiring the Authority to take ownership of a faltering privately owned railroad that linked North Jersey and Manhattan through a Hudson River tunnel.[26] Thus was born the Port Authority Trans-Hudson Corporation or PATH, a high volume rail transit line providing inexpensive access to Manhattan for thousands of North Jersey's daily commuters.[27] Here was further evidence that the perceived power imbalance between the two states was shifting somewhat toward a more favorable outlook for North Jersey.

Another regional development conflict with a different outcome again demonstrated New Jersey's stronger hand in Authority decisions. Faced with growing demand for increased air travel in Greater New York, the Port Authority in the late 1950s explored construction of a new regional airport at a large wetlands site in

North Jersey. Citizen opposition brought gubernatorial resistance and eventual abandonment of the project.[28] Signaling that perhaps the era of large-scale regional economic development projects was nearing an end, the failed project contributed to leadership changes and redirection at the Port Authority.[29] Proof that its regional fortunes were in transition was New Jersey's successful petition in 1972 to rename the agency the Port Authority of New York and New Jersey. Though it seemed to many that New Jersey still needed New York City more than Gotham needed the Garden State, the name change was a symbolic victory for the latter. New Jerseyans could celebrate that, at last, the names of both parties to the union were now on the marriage license.

Meanwhile, by the 1960s the urban crisis plaguing communities across the nation was in full force in North Jersey cities such as Paterson, Elizabeth, Jersey City, Hoboken, and Newark, and in New York City (Map 1, p. 14). All suffered declining economic health and deteriorating physical infrastructure. Poverty, crime and the out-migration of middle-class families, businesses and institutions undermined urban vitality. Strapped for resources, owing in part to diminishing federal support in the 1970s, state and local officials pressed the Authority to play a more direct role in local economic development. Jersey officials questioned why the Authority could build twin 110-story towers in Manhattan, yet not invest in smaller office projects in cities such as Newark. Although the World Trade Center was built in part to serve as the Authority's headquarters, it was also intended to house businesses with regional, national, and international markets. This rationale for the project was lost on North Jersey politicians, and the Authority, responding to pressures for a broader development strategy, reluctantly agreed in the late 1980s to finance construction of an office building in Newark.[30] The precedent thus set, New Jersey gubernatorial pressure induced the Authority to create a bank for regional development. Capitalized by Authority revenue surpluses, the bank was empowered to build local projects in the two states, thus redefining the Authority's earlier definition of the concept of regional benefit. The bank opened the door to greater political influence from the governors of New York and New Jersey, as well as from local officials. In addition, the event seemed to symbolize the Port Authority's departure from large-scale projects of regional benefit.[31] In more recent years the Port Authority has scattered smaller projects such as a resource recovery facility, local industrial parks, and a business park and satellite communications center in the bi-state suburbs.

By the 1990s the public identity of the Port Authority had morphed from the role of builder of heroic proportions to the more or less humdrum role of bi-state landlord over bridges, tunnels, transportation systems, and several million square feet of office and retail space. Having lost, through time and attrition, much of the organizational culture perpetuated by its original cadre of apolitical technocratic professionals, the Authority had to adapt to a changing political climate. With the age of grandiose engineering projects having apparently succumbed to a scarcity of land, growing environmental concerns and not-in-my-backyard civic resistance, New Jersey politicians convinced the Authority to devote more resources to tending local political and public relations vineyards.

SEPTEMBER 11, 2001

Although the Port Authority's balance of power still lies closer to New York than to North Jersey, the fulcrum has shifted somewhat. For example, six members of the Port Authority Board are now appointed by each state's governor and ratified by the appropriate state senate. Power has been further shared through a recent board custom permitting New Jersey to select the board chair, while New York appoints the executive director. Though various issues have arisen over the past fifteen years, nothing matches the aftermath of the destruction of the World Trade Center complex (now termed Ground Zero) on September 11, 2001 (Map 2, p. 22).

To appreciate the resulting irony, it is helpful to recall certain facts. First, New Jersey officials had opposed the Twin Towers project, arguing that it was ill-conceived. Second, once occupied, the towers and other nearby developments became a major employment center for commuters from North and Central Jersey. (Indeed, of the 2,749 casualties in the World Trade Center disaster on September 11, 2001, about 23 percent were from New Jersey).[32] Third, though initially controversial, the towers became, arguably, the defining iconic image of the New York region. Until the 1990s, no other city in the world had twin towers reaching 110 stories. Millions of people in Greater New York, including many North Jerseyans, found civic pride in their symbolism. Ironically, the ugly ducklings, which official New Jersey resisted, became soaring eagles from which many North Jerseyans benefited. In the aftermath of the 2001 terrorist attack on Manhattan, the political climate was altered once again. The death of thirty-seven Port Authority police officers and forty-seven other employees, and the destruction of the agency's headquarters, brought an outpouring of public sympathy for the organization. Its monumental efforts to restore transportation services, replace critical records and infrastructure, and rebuild its highly skilled staff, all the while mourning its catastrophic human losses, put the Port Authority in a sympathetic regional context. Surely, the Authority's organizational personality will emerge altered somewhat by the cataclysmic events ushering the region into the twenty-first century.

Despite its more aggressive role in Port Authority decisions since the 1970s, official New Jersey has raised its voice only selectively in the controversy over the rebuilding of Ground Zero. Showing admirable restraint, New Jersey governors have limited their voices to insisting on a proper monument for the victims and the restoration of PATH train service between Jersey City and Ground Zero. New York leaders such as Governor George Pataki and Mayor Michael Bloomberg, in constrast, have jousted with many interest groups to shape the final redevelopment plan. New Jersey's relative quiescence may have been a tasteful expression of sympathy over politics. Or, it may have been an investment with expectations for future returns when New Jersey needs support from the Authority for a project in its own backyard.

BI-STATE CONFLICT AND COOPERATION

Although it is the oldest regional entity for resolving bi-state differences and building cooperation in Greater New York, the Authority has a limited charter, with many issues falling outside its jurisdiction. Other attempts to create bi-state and tri-state forums for intergovernmental cooperation and coordination have failed. One example is the ill-fated Metropolitan Regional Council, which brought Greater New York leaders together over regional issues from 1956 to 1976, after which it was eliminated.[33] Meanwhile, trans-Hudson contention continues to plague the two states. Three recent examples involve history and prestige, economic development, and tax policy. Underlying all of these, of course, is money.

Throughout the late 1990s New York and New Jersey were involved in a donnybrook over Ellis Island, the Hudson River shrine to American immigration (Map 2). Once owned by New York City, the island was sold to the U.S. government in 1808. The issue, bedeviling bi-state relations for many years, turned on whether New York or New Jersey retained advisory rights to the federal government over a large portion of Ellis Island. Leaders in both states wanted to influence development of the island to foster tourism. They also wanted the prestige and bragging rights associated with the historic site. Located in the Hudson River on the New Jersey side of the state boundary (Map 5, p. 88), the 27.5-acre island lies about one mile from the southern tip of Manhattan but only 1,300 feet from Jersey City.[34] However, when the boundary between the two states was established in 1834, New York retained all rights over the island while New Jersey claimed jurisdiction over the surrounding waters and submerged sections. The issue was further complicated when the original island was enlarged by the addition of several acres of fill between 1898 and 1905. After years of haggling and judicial maneuvering, the issue went before the U.S. Supreme Court.

The *New York Times* ardently editorialized that it would be "an injustice and a threat to sensitive preservation" to split advisory rights over the island between the two states.[35] Moreover, the *Times* continued, arriving immigrants in the nineteenth and early twentieth centuries associated Ellis Island with New York, not New Jersey, thereby undergirding Gotham's claim to dominion.[36] New Jersey readers were reminded that it was not for nothing that the *New York Times* is so named. Though it is widely considered a national and international newspaper, the *Times* displayed what some perceived as a persistent undertone of parochialism about the place of Gotham in the region.

Nonetheless, in 1998 the Supreme Court confirmed that New Jersey rightly claims advisory status over the island's southernmost 24.2 acres, the part created from fill, on which sits about thirty abandoned buildings. New York, it ruled, maintains advisory status over the original 3.3 acres, where the Ellis Island Immigration Museum and Great Hall is located.[37]

Another recent bi-state issue involves the see-saw competition between Manhattan and North Jersey for large-scale real estate development. Throughout most of the twentieth century, Manhattan had the largest concentration of office space in Greater New

York. But, as suburbanization accelerated in the 1970s, many corporations relocated their headquarters or subsidiary offices to outlying Long Island, Connecticut, and New Jersey settings. Corporations and developers adroitly pitted public officials against one another by seeking larger incentives such as tax abatements in return for bringing jobs and tax ratables to their state. In 1996 New Jersey began offering companies willing to move to or expand within the state a ten-year, 80 percent reduction in their annual tax liability. Companies located in New York were then able to coax similar incentives from that city by threatening to move to the suburbs. Dickering had reached new heights of sophistication.

For example, in 1997 the New York-based Standard and Poor's company "shopped" New Jersey for tax relief in exchange for moving its headquarters across the river. A terse confrontation resulted between New Jersey's then-governor, Christie Whitman, and the head of New York's Economic Development Corporation. Standard and Poor's chose to remain in Manhattan, but not before extracting a $34.5 million subsidy from New York's city hall. By early 2003 New Jersey had promised $710 million in subsidies to 280 firms agreeing to expand in or relocate to the state. In Jersey City alone, most of the eight office towers built during the 1990s took advantage of the state's incentive program. Firms such as Merrill Lynch, Morgan Stanley, and J. P. Morgan Chase were among those leasing office space.[38]

Still, state and local economic development incentive programs can backfire. Goldman Sachs, an international investment banking firm, has been headquartered in Manhattan for decades. During the economic boom of the late 1990s, it failed to find an acceptable site in Manhattan to build additional office space. Seeking proximity to the Wall Street area, the bank began building a 42-story office tower across the river (Figure 20, p. 120) on the Jersey City waterfront site of the former Colgate toothpaste manufacturing plant. The $1.3 billion building is emblematic of that city's postindustrial transition from manufacturing to an advanced services center. Connected to Manhattan by the PATH train and ferry service, Jersey City is but minutes from the office canyons of Wall Street. In this case New Jersey offered a ten-year $160 million tax relief incentive to Goldman Sachs.

But the story didn't end there. With the economic recession of 2001–2, the corporation's office space needs shrank and demand from other firms to lease space in the project was less than anticipated. Worse yet, an "insurrection" arose within Goldman Sachs, "by traders who did not want to be cast off to New Jersey."[39] With its Manhattan employees scattered among nine buildings, Goldman Sachs decided to move fewer workers to Jersey City, occupy a smaller space there, and build another tower in Lower Manhattan. Taking advantage of new subsidies resulting from federal and state efforts to rebuild the Ground Zero area of Lower Manhattan, the leaders of Goldman Sachs decided to erect their newest offices on Manhattan's Hudson waterfront directly opposite its Jersey City tower. This saga highlights the extraordinary degree to which some private concerns will go to extract profitable concessions from neighboring jurisdictions when the distance between them can be measured in feet. It also underscores the questionable returns to governments that fight price wars with taxpayer-subsidized incentives, rather than seek cooperative regional agreements to eliminate these self-defeating mechanisms.[40]

A third trans-Hudson issue, involving a payroll tax on commuters who work in New York City, surfaced in 2000. Such a tax had been in force from the mid-1960s until the late 1990s, when New York State's commuters were exempted by their legislature. Upset, Connecticut and New Jersey won a court ruling that the tax was unconstitutional because it was not uniformly levied against all commuters. Not wanting to reinstitute the tax against its own citizens, New York State officials reluctantly rescinded it in 2000, relieving commuters from New Jersey and Connecticut. After September 11, 2001, Mayor Michael Bloomberg sought to offset revenue losses and a dawdling economy by proposing a new commuter tax. He argued that commuters working in New York City, just like residents, should help shoulder the added costs of police, sanitation, and transit services. Bloomberg added that average commuter incomes far exceed average resident incomes. New Jersey politicians raised an outcry and hinted that a retaliatory tax on New Yorkers working in North Jersey was possible. Lack of enthusiasm for the tax from New York Governor George Pataki, as well as bitter opposition from suburban politicians, resulted in the proposal's demise, at least for the time being.[41]

The commuter tax issue shows that not all trans-Hudson bistate bickering is based on *competition for* perceived assets; sometimes it centers on *repulsion of* unwanted liabilities. Another example is solid waste, which has posed an enduring set of problems, especially since crowded New York City has so few disposal sites left within its own borders. During the 1980s medical wastes washed ashore on North and Central Jersey beaches, threatening the state's substantial tourism economy. Already suffering from its gritty image of industrial pollution, the Garden State did not need anything to detract from the appeal of its coastal region. Fingers were pointed at New York City and its troubled solid waste management agency. So concerned were New Jerseyans, their governor appeared in state-sponsored television ads assuring potential visitors that Jersey beaches were clean and safe. Another waste disposal issue surfaced when plans were announced to haul New York City's solid waste to transfer sites in North Jersey. Again, a swift response from New Jersey environmentalists caused New York to back down from the proposal.[42]

In 2000 the Jersey shore became the focal point for another solid waste brouhaha. In this instance, New York was dumping dredge material taken from harbors in Brooklyn and Queens into the ocean off New Jersey's Sandy Hook (Map 2, p. 22). This threatened the Gateway National Recreation Area and Jersey beaches. In spite of an earlier agreement brokered by Al Gore, the nation's vice president at the time, New York failed to establish an upland site for dredge material. Opponents argued that New Jersey had established such sites and that New York was dishonoring its agreement. They charged that the dredge material carried environmental hazards and that once again, North Jerseyans were being treated as though their state was a mere dumping ground for New York's unwanted wastes.

These and other issues betray the underlying conundrum: Greater New York, and especially the Manhattan-North Jersey axis, is one interactive economic region inconvenienced by multiple polities. Employee commuting patterns, capital flows, consumer flows, trade flows, even waste flows—none respects jurisdictional boundaries. Many North Jerseyans *need* Manhattan jobs and *want* Manhattan culture, amusement and entertainment. Many Manhattan employers, businesses, and institutions *need* North Jersey workers, consumers, and products. Like conjoined twins, New York City and North Jersey have a common circulation system. That they are separated by state boundaries and a river seems more a historical accident of geopolitical proportions than a calculated decision based on economic rationality, mutual benefit or convenience. Not surprisingly then, the relationship between municipal, county, and state officials on both sides of the Hudson is characterized by a state of dynamic tension.[43] Trans-Hudson conflicts arise from time to time but do so, it seems, in a climate marked by political relationships running variously from mutually cooperative to mutually exclusive.

Nevertheless, the terms on which bi-state discourse takes place have shifted in recent decades. While the Garden State once suffered from its "long vassalage" to Gotham, today it enjoys a stronger position in bi-state discourse.[44] In part, this position came about through political agency—the deliberate struggle by New Jersey public officials employing the mass media, the judiciary, formal institutions, and informal lines of communication, the better to shape outcomes.[45] The momentum of market forces often underlies political agency, but the sheer weight of shared interests, public opinion, and the constitutionally guaranteed separation of powers between federal and state governments seems to ensure that eventually, for most issues, mutually acceptable resolutions will occur.

Perhaps the second most remarkable feature of this state of dynamic tension is that it has persisted since the seventeenth century. Yet, as Manhattan and North Jersey grew more interdependent over the twentieth century, the nature of their relationship changed. Today, it is not so much goodwill that their leaders pursue; rather, it is the mutual desire to downplay ill will. As Manhattan and North Jersey have become increasingly interdependent economically, the logic of finding politically and economically acceptable compromises has gained momentum. Though cross-border disputes between states (up to and including war) erupt all over the globe, New York and New Jersey exemplify the virtues of civilized, though often messy, diplomacy. Certainly, there is something to celebrate in more than 350 years of such interchange.

CHAPTER TWO

Accommodating Difference at the Extremes of Density and Diversity

Greater New York has long been recognized as the most densely populated metropolitan region in the United States.[1] Among the fifty states, however, New Jersey has persisted as the most densely populated state in the nation for at least the past two decades. Indeed, the entirety of New Jersey's land mass is classified as urban under the U.S. Census Bureau's definition and virtually every community falls within one of the state's Metropolitan Statistical Areas. The overall density in the United States in 2000 was about 80 persons per square mile. By comparison, New Jersey's density (1,134) was about fourteen times the national average and more comparable to nations such as South Korea (1,264) and the Netherlands (1220). Even India (897) and China (354), among the most populous nations on Earth, have densities considerably lower than New Jersey's. Austria, whose population size is comparable to New Jersey's, has about one-fourth the density (255). If the density of the North Jersey suburbs of New York City were merely *similar* to New Jersey's overall density, they would be among the most heavily populated metropolitan suburbs in the United States. But North Jersey's density is about *four times* that of the rest of the state. And, North Jersey's Hudson County

(13,044) is perhaps the most densely populated such unit in the United States outside of New York City.[2]

These figures illustrate the extraordinary intensity of human settlement characterizing life in the Manhattan suburbs of North Jersey. Although life in any metropolitan area requires greater efforts at accommodation among residents than is the case in rural areas, the demands on those who live and work in North Jersey are exceptional by North American terms. To be a resident of the subregion demands an unusual degree of societal cooperation. Congested highways, tightly parked cars, long retail checkout lines, heavily used parks, and smaller yards are only some of the manifestations of North Jersey's close-and-personal lifestyle. Residents who place a high premium on free will and independence are especially challenged. Yet, density is not the only measure of the social character of life. Consider the dizzying array of nationalities, cultures, races, and religions found in the Manhattan suburbs of North Jersey.

DIVERSITY BEFORE THE NINETEENTH CENTURY

Just as it is often associated with crowding and congestion in the popular mind, New Jersey is commonly viewed as an area with a highly diverse population. While this is true, it is especially true of North Jersey. And the state's heterogeneity has been a hallmark of its identity for centuries. It is known that the Lenni Lenape occupied the land for thousands of years before the foreign tones of the Dutch and English languages were heard. Called Delaware Indians by the Europeans, the Lenni Lenape people spoke the Algonkian language. Fishers, hunters, gatherers and farmers, the tribe numbered perhaps a few thousand people when the Dutch arrived. By most European accounts, relations between these aboriginals and the settlers were normally peaceful. However, some infamous episodes of bloodshed, captivity and even slavery on both sides are recorded. Some Dutch settlers were known to be particularly exploitive of the Lenni Lenape, allegedly plying them with alcohol to secure dubious titles to their land.[3]

Yet, even among the Lenni Lenape, there was some degree of diversity. Three separate bands of the tribe have been identified, the most warlike and fearsome of which was the Minsi or Munsee. Living then in what is today North Jersey, their totem was the wolf, a symbol of ferocity; those of the other two bands were more benign animals, the turtle and the turkey. (There is a certain irony in this fact because today's North Jerseyans are widely portrayed as a more aggressive lot than New Jerseyans generally.) As elsewhere in the New World, the newcomers brought disease, liquor, intermarriage, occasional violence, and distinct ideas about the relative sanctity of nature and the rights of property ownership. Through their technology and sheer numbers, the European interlopers prevailed. By the end of the eighteenth century, the Lenni Lenape had all but disappeared from the New Jersey landscape, succeeded as they were by tens of thousands of Europeans, their descendants, and a growing number of African slaves.

In effect, then, the rising numbers of newcomers constituted a second wave of social diversity on the North Jersey landscape. As the historian Richard McCormick noted, eighteenth-century New Jersey quickly became "a colony whose distinguishing mark was to be its heterogeneity."[4] Colonial East Jersey (roughly corresponding to today's North Jersey and the upper Atlantic shoreline) was peopled not only by African slaves and their descendants, but by immigrants from "Holland, Belgium, Finland, France, Germany, Ireland, Scotland, Sweden, and Wales, together with New Englanders and those from England."[5] In less populated West Jersey, English Quakers, Swedes, and Finns were among the nationalities settled along the Delaware River. Even within a single nationality such as the Dutch, the Flemish and Walloons constituted distinct subgroups.[6] Moreover, by the eighteenth century the black population, mostly slaves, had come from the West Indies and Madagascar, as well as Angola and other west African colonies. Some spoke tribal dialects while others spoke a European language.[7] By the end of the Revolutionary War, New Jersey's population of approximately eleven thousand slaves was among the highest of northern states.[8] Although British immigrants were among the most numerous in the original thirteen colonies, New Jersey had perhaps the most diverse population of any New World colony.

This diversity extended even beyond national origins to religion. By the end of the seventeenth century, several Protestant religious communities were scattered about. Among these were Dutch Reformed, Anglicans, Baptists, Puritans, Quakers, and Scotch Presbyterians.[9] By the mid-eighteenth century, one estimate notes, approximately forty Quaker, thirty Dutch Reformed, thirty Baptist, and twenty Anglican congregations had been established in New Jersey, along with smaller groups of Methodists and German or Swedish Lutherans.[10]

By the eighteenth century, McCormick observes, New Jersey already displayed "extraordinary diversity."[11] Perhaps one-half the population was of English descent and more than one-sixth was Scotch, Irish, or Welsh. One-sixth was Dutch, one-tenth was German and the remaining white inhabitants were mostly Swedes and French. Another one-twelfth was of African origin, the vast majority of whom were slaves. [12] Fueling this rich ethnic and racial mixture was the pace of New Jersey's population growth during the eighteenth century. At the century's beginning approximately 15,000 people lived in the state. By 1750 the population had soared to 60,000 and by the eve of the Revolution, to 120,000. Of these, about 60 percent resided in the seven northern counties of the state, which include today's North Jersey.[13]

MULTICULTURALISM, THY NAME IS
NORTH JERSEY

As immigration to the United States surged in the nineteenth century, ethnic and religious diversity accelerated. Fed by the industrial revolution and an explosion of factory labor in the cities of America, the tide of newcomers was nowhere more apparent than in the New York City-New Jersey area. While Ellis Island is commonly associated in the popular mind with New York, the fact that it is much closer to North Jersey ensured that cities such as Hoboken, Jersey City, Newark, and Elizabeth and several smaller towns would become ethnic, racial and religious mosaics. Between 1850 and 1860 the population of Jersey City increased by 300 percent, Newark's by 100 percent, and Bayonne and Passaic by 140 percent each. These and other North Jersey cities would be at the center of the nation's late nineteenth-century industrial revolution. And the Garden State would become known as much for manufacturing plants as for the plants harvested on the state's fruit and vegetable farms. By 1900 four of New Jersey's twenty-one counties—Hudson, Essex, Passaic, and Camden—contained about one-half of the state's population.[14] About one-half of New Jersey's foreign-born population lived in Hudson, Essex, and Passaic counties, while most of the state's remaining non-natives lived in Bergen, Union, and Middlesex counties (Map 2, p. 22). With the exception of Camden, all of these counties are in or adjacent to North Jersey.[15] Thus, over the nineteenth century North Jersey, as part of Greater New York, became one of the most socially diverse subregions in America.

DIVERSITY IN TWENTY-FIRST-
CENTURY NORTH JERSEY

Today, New Jersey continues to sustain an extraordinary variety of people. Almost sixty thousand non-natives became legal immigrants in 2001, followed by nearly fifty-eight thousand in 2002.[16] Spanish-speaking nationalities predominate among all recent immigrants, with more than 1.1 million Hispanics living in the state. Among these, Puerto Ricans are the largest single group, followed by Dominicans, Mexicans, Columbians, and Cubans. Smaller groups include Ecuadorians, Peruvians, Nicaraguans, Costa Ricans, and Salvadorans. At least twenty nationalities contribute to the state's Hispanic population, with northern cities such as Newark, Jersey City, Elizabeth, Paterson and Perth Amboy having large Latino communities.[17] In addition, substantial numbers of migrants from the Asian subcontinent, the Middle East, Eastern Europe, Africa, and the Caribbean islands have further enriched the North Jersey population.

Yet ethnic and racial variety is overlain with income and class differences. A recent study examined incomes of nationalities with at least fifty thousand residents in the state. Filipino households earned the highest median income ($80,946), followed by Chinese ($80,518), and Asian Indians ($75,677). At the lower end were Dominicans ($35,980) and Puerto Ricans ($35,630).[18] As these figures demonstrate though, many non-natives have achieved middle- and upper-middle income security. Thus, New Jersey's fabled diversity extends even to social class.

North Jersey is now undergoing a significant shift in racial and ethnic composition, while at least temporarily reversing the trend of net population decline that bedeviled the subregion over much of the last century. A recent study found that from 2000 to 2002 the five counties comprising North Jersey, plus adjacent Middlesex County, lost 95,143 people to out-migration, while receiving 102,176 from immigration and nearly 53,000 from the net effect of births over deaths.[19] However, the gains have come at a price that includes the loss of older white families. One study estimated that most of the population loss in North Jersey from 2000 to 2002 was accounted for by declines in non-Hispanic whites

CHAPTER 2

($-51,425$), owing largely to deaths and to migration to other states and to other parts of New Jersey. Most of the gains (103,848) were due to increases in minorities such as blacks, Asians, and Hispanics.[20]

But newer immigrants do not completely tell the story of North Jersey's diversity. Although death, migration and intermarriage have somewhat diminished their prominence, the descendents of the predominantly European immigrants of the nineteenth and early twentieth centuries continue to add another dimension. The Census Bureau examined shifts in New Jersey's population for several ancestries for the period 1990 to 2000.[21] Italian Americans are still the largest ethnic group (1,504,000), followed by Irish Americans (1,337,000) and German Americans (1,063,000). Yet, New Jerseyans claiming European ancestry dropped from 6.8 to 5.9 million people between 1990 and 2000. German Americans showed the greatest decline. Though ethnic identity still plays a significant social role in New Jersey, and especially North Jersey, the forces of assimilation continue in dynamic tension with those of ethnic preservation.

What is true of North Jersey's diversity is true of much of the state, in kind if not in degree. Since 1971 New Jersey has consistently ranked fifth behind California, New York, Florida, and Texas in the number of *legal* immigrants it has added annually.[22] That this should be true of the other states is not so surprising, given that they are among the largest in population and land area in America. But with the ninth largest state population and the fifth smallest land area, New Jersey's national ranking of legal immigrants is all the more noteworthy.[23] We should also remember that New Jersey, like other states, has additional numbers of illegal or undocumented aliens. It is no exaggeration then to refer to New Jersey, and especially its northern counties, as among the most elaborately multicultural in North America.[24]

Although there are many racial, ethnic, and religious groups that have suffered discrimination, none have suffered to the extent that the state's African Americans have. Composing 13.6 percent of the statewide population in 2000, New Jersey's blacks only slightly exceed the national share of 12.3 percent.[25] African Americans live throughout the state, especially in cities such as Paterson, Elizabeth, Jersey City, Trenton, and Camden. But they are most heavily concentrated in North Jersey, where in 2000 more than 629,000 African Americans made up nearly 20 percent of the five-county population. Of these, about 327,000 (52 percent) of North Jersey blacks lived in Essex County, primarily in Newark, Orange, East Orange, and Irvington (Map 3, p. 43), with smaller populations in the suburbs of Montclair, Maplewood, South Orange, and West Orange. Like other metropolitan areas, North Jersey consistently registers a high degree of racially segregated residential patterns in national studies.[26] Additionally, many public schools are largely segregated racially, with black children most isolated from whites, Asians, and Hispanics. Although blacks have made significant inroads into some of North Jersey's older suburbs, they are heavily concentrated in the larger cities and have suffered poverty and discrimination at higher rates than most other social groups. Still, many have risen to middle- and upper-middle-class ranks and hold positions of prominence in political, professional, technical, civic, charitable and corporate fields. More so than any other race or ethnic group, African Americans contend with the greatest odds in achieving the American dream. Indeed, their plight represents the litmus test of racial equality and social justice in New Jersey and especially, in North Jersey.[27]

SEEKING THE JUST SOCIETY IN MONTCLAIR

One place where this struggle has reached notable proportions is in the North Jersey town of Montclair (Map 3, p. 43). Settled by

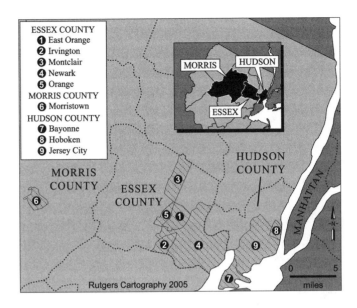

ESSEX COUNTY
❶ East Orange
❷ Irvington
❸ Montclair
❹ Newark
❺ Orange
MORRIS COUNTY
❻ Morristown
HUDSON COUNTY
❼ Bayonne
❽ Hoboken
❾ Jersey City

MORRIS
COUNTY

MORRIS   HUDSON

ESSEX

HUDSON
COUNTY

MORRIS
COUNTY
❻

ESSEX
COUNTY

❸

❺ ❶

❷   ❹   ❾

❽

MANHATTAN

N

0   5

Rutgers Cartography 2005   ❼   miles

Map 3. Hudson, Essex, and Morris counties provide case-study communities illustrating challenges such as achieving equal educational outcomes, reducing racial and ethnic conflict, spurring urban revitalization, and eliminating a legacy of political corruption and organized crime.

Dutch and English immigrants in the late seventeenth century and throughout the eighteenth, the community became a railroad suburb, especially for people working in Newark and Manhattan, in the late nineteenth century. Montclair also became a summer retreat for wealthy urban residents who built large seasonal homes on the hillsides. Over the course of the twentieth century the town emerged as a middle-income haven with the rise of automobile commuting and the construction of a bridge and tunnels spanning the Hudson. Shaped more or less like a narrow upright rectangle, Montclair's northern reaches are known as Upper Montclair, a designation implying as much about social status as geography. Montclair's downtown, with about 150 stores, is aligned along Bloomfield Avenue at the southern edge of the town. Glen Ridge, a socioeconomically comparable town, abuts Montclair's eastern

Figure 1. Busy Bloomfield Avenue is the retail spine of Montclair and connects the town's residents to less affluent communities such as Newark and East Orange.

border and serves as a buffer between Montclair and the blue-collar communities further eastward. In 2000 Montclair's median family income was more than $96,000, or almost twice the U.S. median, and its median housing value was more than $317,000.[28]

Although racial tensions emerged as Montclair's African-American population rose over the late twentieth century, many townspeople strove to forestall white flight. Of the nearly 39,000 residents of Montclair in 2000, 32 percent were African American, 60 percent were white, 3.2 percent were Asian, and 5 percent were Latinos (of any race).[29] Black families are sprinkled throughout most of the town, but the largest concentration lives in the southeastern corner. Over the past few years however, since improvements occurred in the neighborhood's passenger rail service, gentrification has brought competition between whites and minorities for scarce housing.

As North Jersey communities go, Montclair has emerged as

Figure 2. The few publicly subsidized housing units in Montclair have attracted many minority families seeking better schools and safer streets. This complex is next to a commuter train station serving Newark and Manhattan.

one of the most sought-after addresses. A measure of its market appeal is the fact that several celebrities have settled in the town. Major league athletes, such as Yogi Berra, the former Yankee catcher, and actresses such as Meryl Streep and Olympia Dukakis, have called Montclair home. Many creative people, including actors, artists, dancers, musicians, composers, writers, and poets, are residents. Numerous films, television shows, and commercials have been shot on location in Montclair to take advantage of its picture-book image. The town boasts a university, four local theater companies, four movie houses, an arts theater, and two jazz clubs. More than fifty restaurants and eateries draw residents and visitors alike.

Beyond these attributes, what is the appeal of the town? Most people seem attracted to Montclair's varied housing stock, environmental quality, access to Manhattan, and school system. Dwellings range from apartments and condominiums to town-

Figure 3. A few predominantly African American neighborhoods such as this one are located along lower Bloomfield Avenue. They contain most of the moderate-income housing remaining in Montclair.

houses, Victorians, Dutch Colonials, English Tudors, Georgian Revival mansions, and a smattering of contemporary mega-mansions. Competition among homebuyers is keen and Montclair consistently sustains among North Jersey's highest average home prices. Mature trees abound, small fortunes are invested in home landscaping, historic buildings are carefully preserved, and eighteen parks exist in or near the town. Daily train service to Manhattan, Hoboken, and Jersey City transports neurosurgeons, hedge fund managers, certified public accountants, journalists, advertising executives, and others of nearly every professional stripe.

Given its affluence, it is not surprising that Montclair's reputation for quality education is one of its most popular features. It is not Garrison Keillor's mythical Lake Wobegon, but the town and its relentless emphasis on education gives the impression that every child *really is* above average. Nearly all graduates of its high school and two private schools go on to higher education.

Figure 4. Upper Montclair, considerably north of the Bloomfield Avenue retail corridor, has its own rail commuter stations and shopping areas, putting distance between wealthier and poorer residents.

Regardless of class or race, many families live in Montclair to send their children to its highly rated public school system. But for their educational backgrounds, many residents could not have achieved the successes in life necessary to have a Montclair address. For their children therefore, there will be no compromises.

For all the good will implicit in the town's reputation for social justice, the reality is that interracial parity is a good deal more difficult to achieve and maintain than many suspected. Part of the problem is that social class matters. Children from less privileged families, regardless of race, are less likely to receive the parental help with schoolwork typical in more fortunate households. Their parents (especially single parents) often work long hours to make ends meet and are less likely to attend school events. Poor children are more likely to be stigmatized by the clothes, material goods, privileges, and home environments of their affluent classmates. In some cases, teachers and administrators, consciously or subconsciously, treat these children less favorably or show lower expectations for them. Although disparities in average income exist between blacks and whites, sizeable variations occur among blacks themselves. More affluent black children sometimes contend with the taunts of their poorer racial counterparts, who ridicule them for their discipline and accomplishments. These and other factors have shown that even Montclair, with all of its resources, collective intelligence, good will, and sophistication, has not yet reached the promised land.

As noble as Montclair's efforts have been, there are still persistent problems of trust between blacks and whites. Periodically, doubts arise among African American parents when a proposed school budget reduction appears to affect their children disproportionately. Fears of white flight emerge when some white parents transfer their children from public to private schools, claiming they are not sufficiently challenged in racially mixed classrooms. Specialized curricula in fields such as science or the arts have been offered at individual schools in efforts to attract a mixed racial profile; but if too many whites or blacks apply for admission, some must be denied, causing displeasure.[30] And, school officials struggle with the conundrum that though they may spend equally on black and white children, differential achievement results bring cries from some families for higher expenditures on black children.

Moreover, social conditions further color the climate of interracial trust in the town. For example, lunchtime co-mingling is uncommon at school and children tend to sit with others of their own race. (Indeed, white and black parents themselves report little interracial social interaction with their friends and neighbors.) When African American children visit neighborhood stores at lunch or after school, some report that they are more likely to be singled out by store clerks fearful of pilfering.[31]

Doubtless, Montclair residents harbor every shade of attitude

Figure 5. Montclair's summer public school programs attract large numbers of minority students. Many parents enroll their children, hoping to increase the children's opportunities for advancement in the future.

Figure 6. Montclair's private academies have offered a refuge to middle- and upper-income students whose families are dissatisfied with the community's public schools.

toward the town's interracial goals, from quietly resistant to evasively ambivalent to stridently enthusiastic. But for many residents, to live in Montclair (or similar nearby communities such as Maplewood and South Orange) is to make a declaration, however modestly, about personal values. Although communities such as Montclair have not eliminated racial misunderstanding and distrust, they are at the forefront of racial justice in suburban America.[32] Perhaps then, it can be said of Montclair's school system what has been said of democratic government; it is the worst system on Earth, except for all the rest.

NEITHER MELTING POT NOR CAULDRON OF CONTENTION

North Jersey has an extremely diverse demographic profile that is further challenged by a level of population density perhaps unmatched by other metropolitan suburbs of its geographical scale. In that respect it is most representative of the Greater New York region of which it is a part. And much like residents of New York City, most residents of North Jersey routinely exhibit a standard of tolerance and good will among themselves that, while not unimpeachable, is admirable by most standards. To be sure, progress has come in fits and starts and there have been many events over the years that have tested egalitarian ideals. It is clear, then, that North Jersey's highly multicultural society is a work in progress. If it has not become a true melting pot, however, neither can it be called a seething cauldron of discord.

CHAPTER THREE

Competing for Space and Resources
in the Land of Localism

In many respects, North Jersey serves as a transitional zone of Greater New York. As such, one of its metropolitan roles is to mediate conflicts over space and resources as growth pushes outward from one of the largest, densest, and most socially diverse central cities on Earth. As development has spread fan-like through and later, beyond, the five counties closest to Manhattan, it has extended the reach of Greater New York to large areas of the state and into southern New York State and eastern Pennsylvania (Map 2, p. 22). Sheer growth itself in an area of diminishing space and resources poses substantial problems. But North Jersey's urbanization, and the disintegration of traditional relationships between older cities and newer suburbs, places additional burdens on the ecosystem. Through the dynamics of supply and demand, markets order space and rationalize the allocation of resources, but they seldom effectively address larger social and environmental challenges. Thus, governance and the political process have been pressed into the breach in response to increasingly strident conflicts. As a consequence, there are troubling signs that North Jersey is as close to the precipice of unsustainability as perhaps any metropolitan subregion in North America.

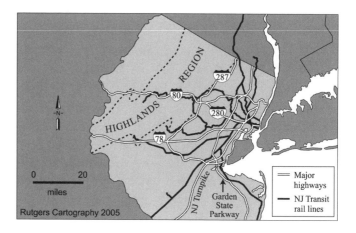

Map 4. North Jersey is stitched together by a dense web of transportation corridors, including extensive interstate highways and passenger rail service. Now the pristine Highlands region is threatened by encroaching development.

RUNNING OUT OF LIVING SPACE IN NORTH JERSEY

Although early twentieth-century urbanization and suburbanization were already extensive in several North Jersey communities, not until after World War II did the pressures of the baby boom, rapid suburban housing development, and vehicular proliferation raise daunting challenges.[1] Highways were becoming more congested, parking opportunities were increasingly limited, and schools were overcrowded. State highway spending and the Federal Aid Highway Act of 1956 brought some relief in the form of millions of dollars worth of concrete and macadam. The opening of the New Jersey Turnpike (1951–52), a link in I-95, and the Garden State Parkway (1955) connected North Jersey to Central Jersey, the Jersey shore, and the Philadelphia suburbs (Map 4). Residential subdivisions, strip retail development, and the state's first regional shopping centers soon appeared at various interchanges. As development pressures continued into the 1970s, Interstates 280 (1947–80), 80 (1951–73), and 78 (1956–89) evolved in segments, providing an east-west orientation for new growth and complementing the existing north-south pattern along the Turnpike and Parkway. Eastern Pennsylvania and western New Jersey were now linked by high-speed highways to Greater New York. Tying the east-west and north-south corridors together was I-287, segments of which opened over the period of 1958 to 1994.

White flight, or the outflow of white households from North Jersey cities such as Paterson, Newark, Jersey City, Hoboken, and Elizabeth, began as a trickle even before the end of World War II. As blacks, Puerto Ricans and other minorities moved into these places after the war, however, the trickle became a flood. Fears about falling home values, increasing crime, and the loss of friends and neighbors to the suburbs caused a forest of "for sale" signs to sprout. City halls struggled to stem the tide, using federal Urban Renewal funds to demolish so-called slums and blighted areas and build new quarters, primarily for business and institutional use. Over the second half of the twentieth century, hundreds of thousands of young "starter" families relocated to the new residential enclaves, forming a growing arc to the north, west, and south of North Jersey's Manhattan suburbs.

During the 1950s and 1960s federal and state programs spurred suburban governments to develop master plans and create or update zoning ordinances. Over the 1970s and 1980s state and federal agencies struggled to increase environmental criteria in the planning process. Yet, urban sprawl continued to consume enormous swaths of former farmland and forest in the Garden State. One dismissive observer of national land use trends typified New Jersey's formerly rural areas as a "nightmare landscape of freeways, malls, and jive plastic commuter dormitories."[2] By the mid-1980s it was apparent to many New Jerseyans that local governments were not effective on their own and that greater state authority was needed. While comprehensive planning had been the rallying cry of the 1970s, statewide growth management became the next line of defense in the 1980s.

It was perhaps a measure of how critical the growth issue had become in New Jersey that the state became only the third in the continental United States to enact a statewide growth management law.[3] Among other goals the new law encouraged closer coordination between county and municipal planning processes and pressured local governments to prepare master land use plans. But these measures alone could not control sprawl, in part because the state government never provided adequate regulatory powers to localities or to its own agencies. Nor did it help fund adequate infrastructure to serve new suburban populations. Further challenging planners were the state supreme court's pioneering Mt. Laurel decisions, which sought to increase affordable suburban housing.[4] Precedents set by these cases provided that developers could sue certain suburban municipalities for failing to zone land for higher density moderate-income housing. Many communities were motivated primarily by desires to maintain demographic homogeneity, while others claimed inadequate school space or street and highway capacity to accommodate large numbers of new households. Consequently, many towns spent years in costly litigation or accepted large increases in housing density to forgo such expenses.[5]

By the mid-1990s the new bromide among states such as New Jersey was "smart growth." The state prepared a statewide map that generally encouraged new construction in built-up areas such as cities, older suburbs and the edges of smaller towns. Farmland, watersheds, wetlands and other open or environmentally sensitive areas would receive more stringent restrictions on development. James McGreevy, then the governor, demonstrated strong leadership in advancing his smart growth policies. He argued that about fifty acres of land per day, or more than eighteen thousand acres per year, are lost to development in New Jersey. Several studies underscored his warning. For example, a 2003 report identified conversion of undeveloped land as the greatest threat to the quality of life in New Jersey. It found that water supplies and wildlife habitat were both suffering from urban sprawl.[6] One reason surely is that there is so little land left to accommodate new growth. Statistics prepared by the U.S. Department of Agriculture show that of all of the states in 1997, New Jersey was the most extensively developed. Thirty-nine percent of its land area was developed, while in the runner-up states, Massachusetts and Rhode Island, development covered 30 percent. Meanwhile, a U.S. Bureau of the Census study estimated that New Jersey's population grew from 8.4 to 8.6 million from 2000 to 2002. Most of the projected growth occurred in North and Central Jersey, along the Atlantic coast, and in a thin belt across the Delaware River from the Philadelphia area. Only South Jersey remained relatively unchanged, according to the study.[7]

Some observers in New Jersey estimate that build-out will be reached in less than twenty years, especially if population grows by a projected one million people by 2020. Developers insist that the state's smart growth policy of diverting new construction away from undeveloped areas and into existing communities is unrealistic, given market demand for open space, low crime, effective schools, and other facets of the American dream.[8]

NORTH JERSEY'S LAST FRONTIER

As growth has pushed outward from the nearby North Jersey suburbs of Manhattan, it has encompassed large parts of Morris, Warren and Sussex counties, among others. The scenic Highlands lie in the direct path of development and are part of a resource covering sections of four states (Map 4, p. 52). Research in 2002 on the New York and New Jersey sections of the Highlands revealed that an average of 3,700 acres per year was lost to development from 1984 to 1995. From 1995 to 2000 the rate of consumption rose to 5,200 acres per year. Though approximately 1.4 million people live in the four-state Highlands region, more than one-half of them reside in the ninety-four municipalities within the North Jersey section.[9] But space is not the only issue in the Highlands. About one-half of state residents receive their drinking water from Highlands watersheds.[10] Thus, many people view this fragile area as the last frontier of scenic and environmentally open space left in North Jersey. In recognition, the state enacted a law in 2004 that provided special planning and review procedures for approximately one-half of the 800,000-acre region.[11] Highly controversial, the new law will be one more test of the resolve of state officials and environmentalists in the face of opposition from a powerful real estate industry, some town officials and disgruntled landowners.

RUNNING OUT OF SPACE

One reason for such doubts is a kind of collective ambivalence among state citizens. A recent survey of New Jerseyans found that more than 80 percent of the respondents complained of declining open space, rising traffic congestion, and urban sprawl. But there was no clear consensus about how government should respond. Those surveyed were about evenly split on whether limiting new development or protecting private property rights was more important. Almost one-half of the respondents said they would support further restrictions on housing construction in undeveloped areas, but 40 percent were opposed. Moreover, 60 percent favored relinquishing some of their community's local control over development (to higher authorities at the county or state level), if such a measure could preserve more open space; but 31 percent opposed the idea.[12] Thus, though sentiment that New Jersey should retard growth seems to be widespread, a substantial minority still appear unwilling to accept changes necessary to control development. Generally, citizens seem to show more support for home-rule control over land use than for economic growth, jobs, tax base, or income. Whatever the general sentiment is across the state, it is likely that feelings about these issues are stronger among North Jerseyans.

Rather than try to achieve smart growth objectives strictly through regulations, many states have convinced landowners to voluntarily sell agricultural, timber and environmentally sensitive lands. It is ironic that, though calling itself the Garden State, New Jersey has less than ten thousand farms, among the smallest number in any state in America. As if to underscore this point, the U.S. Department of Agriculture announced that between 1997 and 2002, the state lost 51,227 acres of farmland.[13] New Jersey's open space program purchased almost 300,000 acres of farmland and forest for recreational use and environmental protection between 1998 and 2003.[14] Yet, even a program so seemingly benign as open space acquisition has become captive to the ongoing competition for resources between urban and suburban politicians. In 2003 Democrats from a few urban districts held the program hostage in the state legislature until expenditures from the open space fund were designated to finance the repair of inner-city parks.[15]

WILDLIFE

Citizen complaints about traffic congestion, crowded schools, and disappearing open space are one measure of the state's growth conundrum. Another measure comes from growing evidence that humans and other species are in increasing contention for living space. Nothing so emphasizes this point as a 300-pound black bear clawing at one's kitchen door. Such human-animal confrontations have become increasingly common in areas of North Jersey. Nearly a century ago only an estimated one hundred of these bears were still living in the state.[16] For many years black bear sightings were infrequent in New Jersey. By 2003, however, stronger restrictions on bear hunting, reductions in polluted biosystems, and a growing supply of food from proliferating household and restaurant disposal containers had raised the bear population to an estimated fifteen hundred. Although suburbanization drove the bruins toward the wooded Highlands for a time, eventually many lost their natural fear of humans as contact increased. The animals began to migrate southward and eastward, foraging for food in smaller towns and newer suburban subdivisions. Though the bears are rarely aggressive toward humans, there have been several incidents of home and car break-ins and backyard visits as the animals search through garbage and other food sources. Several dozens have been killed by vehicles; many others were killed by state authorities when other methods of removal were not feasible.

Though once environmentalists worried that black bears would become extinct, the species has learned how to adapt to rising human population and declining habitat. With only very restricted hunting allowed, they have gradually increased their numbers. But unlike bears in less populated states, Jersey bruins, with Darwinian certitude, have begun to produce cubs at an earlier age than normal, leading to more litters in a female bear's lifetime. Like some teenagers, Jersey bears appear to be "advanced for their age" and thus engage in more sexual activity.[17] Some animals, such as the notorious "Bob the Bear," have become repeat offenders and are trapped, released elsewhere, and trapped again, in a cycle of obstinate ursine recidivism. In their migration out of the Highlands, black bears increased their presence in the state from 48 towns in 1995 to 140 in 2001.[18] Though New Jersey was perhaps the last state experts expected to hold a major conference on the black bear, it happened in 2003 when the state hosted the first meeting in thirty-four years of the Eastern Black Bear Workshop.[19] That same year the state government reluctantly authorized the state's first bear hunt in more than thirty years, resulting in 328 animals killed. In 2005 another hunting season yielded nearly 300 dead bears. Throughout, the issue has drawn ardent opponents and proponents of hunting as a means of controlling the bear population.

But bears are not the only species in abundance. Local and state officials have struggled for years over the rising population of deer in North and Central Jersey. Like the bears, the deer have learned to adapt to humans, increasing their numbers significantly even as the supply of suitable habitat is whittled away by the bulldozers and backhoes of creeping suburbanization. Deer, of course, are less threatening to humans, although they do feed on gardens and decorative plants and pose a danger to drivers. Like that of the bear, the deer population has expanded in part because the culture of hunting has diminished in the state as farming has succumbed to spreading population. State and local officials have tried trapping and transferring deer to rural areas but this tactic has brought little success in reducing their suburban numbers. Many people oppose the hunting of bear and deer on the grounds that it is inhumane and because weapons discharges threaten people living in populated areas. Birth control measures are favored by some, but experiments have shown that, while effective, this method is expensive and labor intensive. Thus few communities have hired professional hunters to cull their deer herds with the hope that their expertise will eliminate the threat to humans.

Canada geese have become a third wildlife problem for large areas of the state. Normally a seasonal migratory bird, many Canada geese live in New Jersey year-round, thriving on farmland, golf courses and corporate and municipal parks. Current federal regulations restrict the killing of Canada geese. New Jersey, with approximately 95,000 nesting geese, is estimated to have the greatest concentration of such birds in the United States. Though they pose no direct danger to human beings, the birds deposit many tons of droppings, bringing inconvenience and potential sanitation problems and polluting the state's limited water sources.[20]

Even though bear, deer and Canada geese have increased their numbers, many plants and animals on the state's endangered or threatened species lists could disappear. Whether increasing or decreasing in numbers, however, some species are struggling with their natural limits of adaptability, challenged by spreading urbanization. In the case of bear, deer, and geese, adaptation has come through the animals' extension of their habitats into towns, suburbs, and exurbs. These uncharacteristic patterns might better be viewed as a last-ditch attempt to find accommodation with man, the most formidable obstacle to their survival. If efforts to preserve North Jersey's few remaining wildlife habitats fail, people may someday have to be content to experience some native wildlife species in zoos, preserves and greenhouses. For in a contest between humans and wildlife, humans usually win.

WATER

Periodic seasonal droughts pose another growth-related problem. In 2002, for example, state officials watched nervously as reservoir levels, especially in North Jersey, dropped precipitously and water rationing was imposed. With time the emergency abated as rain and snow replenished supplies. Yet, as the population increases in New Jersey, especially North Jersey, the margin of safety grows slimmer between water supply and demand. Periodic water shortages could once be tolerated because backup supplies allowed residents to wait out seasonal variations in precipitation. With more visitors, more workers, more residents and more consumption per person, New Jersey pushes ever closer to the natural limits of its own growth capacity. But sheer water consumption is not the only dilemma facing the state. Stormwater runoff from farms, golf courses, corporate parks, and lawns deposits tons of nitrogen, phosphates, and toxic residues from fertilizers and pesticides in New Jersey waterways. Runoff from highways, parking lots, driveways, building rooftops, and industrial and commercial businesses such as petroleum refineries and filling stations inject contaminants into the ecosystem. Heavy metals such as lead and mercury and chemical distillates such as polyaromatic hydrocarbons, polychlorinated biphenyls, and tetrachloreoethylene threaten people and wildlife.[21] In 2002 the state's Department of Environmental Protection announced that 42 percent of state residents drew their household supplies from groundwater sources such as wells. A substantial number of groundwater sites, more than twelve thousand, were contaminated.[22]

Water supply and quality for human consumption are particularly poignant issues in North Jersey. And, as is so often the case, they have brought political clashes. Both Newark and Jersey City have no watersheds within their own boundaries. Instead, both cities rely on exurban and rural watersheds for their water supply. Although the city of Newark owns much of the land in the watershed from which it draws its drinking water, the land is located in several suburban jurisdictions north of the city. In 1989 when the state enacted a moratorium on land development in watersheds, Newark sued for a reduction in the property taxes it paid to these jurisdictions. Though Newark was a prime beneficiary of the building moratorium, and though it could not develop its own watershed holdings, city hall argued that land values were diminished and that tax valuations should be reduced accordingly. The court's verdict won Newark a 30 percent reduction in net taxes owed to the suburban jurisdictions. Jersey City, in a similar situation, soon benefited from Newark's judicial challenge.

This case framed water supply issues in terms of urban Democrats in conflict with suburban Republicans. Forced by state law to forgo some Newark and Jersey City property tax revenues, the upset suburban jurisdictions petitioned the state legislature for relief, calling for the state treasury to offer compensation. Seeking to keep the peace, legislators approved a revised proposal and the money began flowing in 1997 and 1998. However, in 2002 the governor, a Democrat, suspended the program, citing the state's budget woes. This raised partisan suspicions among some of the predominantly Republican watershed towns.[23] Continuing state budgetary deficits have stalled reinstitution of the compensation program, causing the suburban jurisdictions to raise taxes, cut services or both. Once again, urban and suburban jurisdictions are at loggerheads.

AFFORDABLE HOUSING

The state's thirty-year-old affordable housing program is another case of urban and suburban interests at odds. Relatively high land costs and restrictive zoning discourage construction of homes for low-, moderate-, and lower-middle-income households. For these and other reasons, suburban housing that is affordable to teachers, fireman, police officers, starter families, immigrants, single-wage earners, and other moderate-income households is often in short supply.

The state's Council on Affordable Housing (COAH) is charged with establishing quotas of affordable housing for rapidly growing New Jersey communities.[24] COAH was formed by the legislature in response to the New Jersey Supreme Court's Mt. Laurel decisions in 1975, 1983, and 1986. Officials in these towns are challenged to zone land sufficiently to allow their quota to be filled. When a community fails to do so, developers are empowered to bring suit to override local zoning restrictions. COAH's goal is a ratio wherein one out of every four housing units built in these municipalities is affordable to people of moderate incomes. Ironically, developers and affordable housing advocates, normally strange bedfellows, sometimes join forces to sue communities to live up to their COAH-mandated affordable housing quotas. If they succeed, builders are allowed to construct more housing units, thereby increasing profit margins, while housing advocates secure an increase in affordable units.

However, a highly controversial provision allows suburban jurisdictions to buy out part of their responsibility much the way that wealthy young men once escaped military conscription when their families paid other men to take their place. COAH rules allow suburban communities to reduce up to 50 percent of their affordable housing quota by donating a sum of money to a nearby city such as Newark or Paterson. The cities are required to spend the funds, termed Regional Contribution Agreements (RCAs), on building affordable housing within their own borders. Thus, though the supply of new affordable housing in the state is increased through RCAs, the original purpose of the Mt. Laurel decisions—increasing the supply of suburban affordable housing—is diminished. Affordable housing advocates have mounted judicial challenges to RCAs, but to date their actions have found little support.[25]

By 2003 about 37,000 moderately priced units had been built since New Jersey's affordable housing program began in 1986.[26] Critics argue that, by requiring communities to accept more housing units at greater densities than their zoning allows, the program contributes to urban sprawl and traffic congestion. Defenders counter that the program reduces economic segregation and enhances access to better housing, employment and educational opportunities for moderate-income families. The affordable housing problem is especially acute in North Jersey, where demand is high and vacant land is scarce. Thus, COAH is another example of how the state government must intervene to seek accommodation between city and suburban interests.

CRUSTAL URBANIZATION

In the five counties of Inner North Jersey no single central place has historically served as the economic and population center of the sub-region. Instead, North Jersey is polycentric, with four central cities. Elizabeth, Paterson, Jersey City, and Newark range in population from about 120,000 to 273,000 (Map 1, p. 14). The communities are in relatively close proximity to one another and they compete to attract population, investment, and jobs. Additionally, in the interstices among the cities are many smaller industrial communities such as Kearny, Hackensack, Union City, Bayonne, Passaic, and Hoboken. Moreover, older suburban towns such as Westfield, Plainfield, Montclair, South Orange, Wayne, Tenafly, and Paramus cluster nearby. Together, these communities constitute a sprawling, amoeba-like "crust" consuming much of the topography of North Jersey. As such, this pattern of "crustal urbanization," as I call it, undermines the traditional sense of centrality common in cities all over the world.[27] Crustal urbanization should not be confused with suburban sprawl, the distinguishing characteristic of which is inefficient, low-density development patterns. Crustal urbanization is substantially unbroken and occurs at building and population densities considerably in excess of those associated with sprawl.

Suppose that North Jersey had developed in a more conventional unicentric urban pattern such as Cleveland, Baltimore, or Cincinnati. If the year 2000 populations of Elizabeth, Paterson, Jersey City, and Newark were combined into a single city, the population would be just over 783,000.[28] Although this figure represents about 9 percent of New Jersey's total population, it is comparable to the year 2000 populations of the nation's twelfth- and thirteenth-largest cities—Indianapolis (782,000) and San Francisco (777,000), respectively.[29]

Yet, the metropolitan implications of a more conventional development pattern in North Jersey are even more impressive. Combining the urban and suburban populations of Bergen, Essex, Hudson, Passaic, and Union counties (Map 2, p. 22) would yield a combined 2000 population of 3.3 million.[30] This figure exceeds the total 2000 population of the Minneapolis-St. Paul MSA (nearly 3 million) and is similar to those of the Phoenix-Mesa MSA (3.2 million), the Boston-New Hampshire PMSA (3.4 million), and the Dallas PMSA (3.5 million). Such a North Jersey metropolis would be exceeded in population by only ten metropolitan areas, including New York, Los Angeles, Chicago, Philadelphia, Houston, and Atlanta.[31]

Of course, sheer population size is not the issue. Rather, it is the combination of a single large metropolitan region centered on a single central city. For example, suppose North Jersey had grown as the Pittsburgh, St. Louis or Louisville regions grew. The resulting metropolis might have offered a better counterbalance to the economic vortex created by New York City, against which Newark, Jersey City, Elizabeth, and Paterson have historically competed for economic and cultural opportunities. It is at least an arguable proposition that the sheer lack of a single dominant central city or metropolitan area in North Jersey has complicated many things, including the development of a unified political power base in the state capital.[32] Instead of concordant voices representing a common set of place-based interests, North Jersey's crustal urbanization encourages competition among urban and suburban communities for state and federal subsidies, charitable donations, private investment, jobs, housing, and revenues.

Furthermore, crustal urbanization discourages municipal efficiency in the provision of utilities and services and the awarding of contracts. Indeed, "place matters," but the physical character of places may matter even more in achieving regional political cooperation.[33]

POST-SUBURBANIZATION

The situation is further muddied by trends over the past three or four decades. Sometimes termed post-suburbanism, these trends have brought about a gradual disconnection between traditional or nuclear cities and their surrounding suburban regions.[34] Throughout the first half of the twentieth century traditional suburbanization resulted in a degree of mutual dependency between central cities and their suburbs. These cities depended on suburbanites for part of their employment and tax base, while suburbanites depended on the cities for their livelihood and for some shopping and entertainment opportunities. In some cases, the suburbs purchased services such as sewer and water from city agencies. During the latter half of the last century, however, as suburbanization spread further away from the cities and their older suburbs, these historic linkages deteriorated. Postsuburbanites live in far-flung, loosely structured communities and are largely, if not entirely, dependent on motor vehicles to shop, work, attend school, recreate, and run errands. Workplaces are located along highways in office parks or corporate campuses and shopping generally occurs in malls and strip developments. Convenient mass transit and sidewalks connecting homes to shopping are rare. Instead of the suburban-to-central-city commuting patterns common in the postwar decades, today's postsuburbanites trace a formless maze of trails, many of which converge on outlying communities with large corporate employers.[35]

One symptom of post-suburbanism is the emergence of "edge

cities," a term popularized by Joel Garreau.[36] By conventional terms, edge cities are not really cities at all; rather, they are large complexes of commercial, office, and residential development loosely tied together by highways. Typically, they are connected to a regional shopping mall and contain office towers, nearby retail strips, and housing subdivisions, including gated communities. Yet, according to Garreau, edge cities support traditional functions associated with conventional nuclear cities, such as work, leisure, and shopping. But the range of racial, ethnic, and social class interaction is much narrower, in part because there are few sidewalks or other public places where people of widely varying backgrounds can come into casual contact. Privately controlled spaces reign in the edge city. Post-suburbanism, then, results largely in the severing of social and economic interrelationships between urban and suburban residents. At the same time, the heavy dependence in edge cities on motor vehicles also contributes to energy consumption, regional air pollution, and traffic congestion.

GOVERNMENTAL FRAGMENTATION AND GRANULATION

Crustal urbanization and post-suburbanism are two dynamics by which local governments and markets have accommodated the tensions between North Jersey's enormous population density and social diversity and its diminishing land and resources. But there is a third element to the story. As populations have pushed outward from the largest cities, especially during the late nineteenth century and throughout the twentieth, the incorporation of new municipalities such as boroughs, townships, and cities proceeded at a rampant pace. Some observers attribute New Jersey's penchant for small-town localism to New Englanders who migrated during the colonial era.[37] Whatever the source, the "pro-

liferation of postage-stamp boroughs," driven in part by the com-
forts of home rule, tells us much about how New Jerseyans have
adapted to the state's extraordinary social diversity and to its
extraordinary population concentration.[38] Today, New Jersey has
21 counties, 566 local governments, and 552 school districts. The
appeal of numerous, small government units is that their leaders
are more accessible to voters and their official proceedings are
more difficult to camouflage from public scrutiny. Citizens find
public meetings smaller and less intimidating and public officials
easier to approach. In short, many people find small governments
to be more responsive. And, it takes a smaller number of voters
to influence official decisions.

For many New Jerseyans, and especially North Jerseyans,
smaller is better. Historically lenient state incorporation laws
have made it relatively easy for citizens to de-annex a portion of
an existing municipality and create a smaller one over which they
have more control. Doing so husbands tax resources to pay for
high-priority matters such as better schools or police protection.

Offsetting these virtues, critics argue, are the inefficiencies of
numerous small governments each paying to maintain a school
system, town hall administration, and police and fire depart-
ments. They cite the economies possible with larger governmental units and the opportunities to enhance social diversity. Critics
say that governmental fragmentation permits political fragmentation and serves as a *modus operandi* for advancing the compart-
mentalization of small group interests.[39] One outcome of this
pattern in North Jersey is the subregion's extreme racially segregated housing patterns.[40] Despite the Mt. Laurel court decisions,
local government zoning and land regulation ordinances have led
to racial and socioeconomic exclusion in many areas by limiting
development of affordable housing.[41] Heavy local government reli-
ance on property tax revenues encouraged many municipalities

to "zone in" only middle- and upper-income housing and in some cases, tax-generous commercial development.[42] Balkanization has also permitted local governments to shield more of their local revenues, preventing state governments from redistributing resources in order to serve statewide social and environmental purposes more equitably.[43]

How severe a problem is governmental fragmentation in North Jersey? Communities in the Garden State average less than 15 percent the size of those nationally in terms of land area. Similarly, the average New Jersey county is less than one-third the size of counties across the nation. This situation is even more pronounced in North Jersey, where local governments and counties average roughly one-third the size of those in New Jersey overall.[44] By these measures, then, the dilemma in North Jersey is not mere fragmentation but rather *government granulation*. To be sure, governmental granulation is part of a larger pattern in Greater New York. And, indeed, it has been well established for many years, according to earlier studies. Even nationwide studies recognize the detrimental effects of local government balkanization.[45]

Federal, state, and local antidiscrimination laws covering housing, employment, school assignments, and racial profiling have attempted to offset some of the divisive effects of granulated government, crustal urbanization, and post-suburbanism. But these forces result from both market trajectories and political agency; together, they demonstrate the constraints on true social assimilation.[46] Land and government thus have served in New Jersey—and especially in its northern counties—to mediate conflict among different races, ethnicities, and social classes; they have done so by permitting the accommodation of extraordinary human differences at the subregional scale while promoting patterns of separation at the county and municipal scales.

ETHNIC CONFLICT AND POST-
SUBURBANISM IN MORRISTOWN

Morristown, like Montclair, is considered by some outsiders to be a bastion of white affluence (Map 3, p. 43). In truth, the picture is more complicated. Located a half-hour's drive due west of Montclair, Morristown's 2000 population was slightly more than 18,000. What distinguishes the two towns is that Montclair is a predominantly Democratic stronghold in a county controlled by Democrats; Morristown, in contrast, is a predominantly Democratic stronghold in a county controlled by Republicans. Thus, black and poor families in Montclair have sympathetic voices from towns such as Newark, East Orange and Orange in Essex County. Their counterparts in Morristown however, are far outnumbered by white Morris County Republicans with somewhat different priorities.

Over the past three decades, as population in North Jersey has spread westward and southward into Morris, Sussex, Warren, Hunterdon, and Somerset counties, the Morristown area has served as a gateway for suburban growth. As such, the town is located at the epicenter of what might be termed Outer North Jersey. Nearby communities such as Madison, Chatham, Mendham, Basking Ridge, and Bernardsville are bastions of wealth and comfort. Crustal urbanization has not yet welded these towns together, separated as they are by horse farms, public parks, nature preserves, hillside forests, and verdant dells. North and west of Morristown the Highlands serve as a buffer against sprawl and residents hope that newly imposed state growth controls there will preserve the town's scenic surroundings.

Morristown has long enjoyed a historic identity. Settled in 1703, its former inhabitants include George Washington, Alexander Hamilton, Samuel F. B. Morse (co-inventor of the telegraph), and Thomas Nast (the celebrated political cartoonist). At Morris-

Figure 7. Morristown's settlers included New Englanders, who left their mark in the form of a beautiful town common known locally as "the Green." Surrounded by shops, offices, and churches, this historic space dates to the early eighteenth century.

town's center is the Green, a landscaped New England-style town common, popular with homeless people, biker clubs, Latino families, and the white-collar lunch crowd. Several restaurants, shops, and a community theater draw substantial visitors to Morristown. Hundreds of weekday commuters to Manhattan, Hoboken, and Jersey City converge on the train station or express bus stops. Town, county, and corporate offices draw thousands of workers and contribute to the town's healthy tax base.

Gothic revival, Queen Anne, shingle-style, Eastlake, and colonial revival houses ring the town center. Here and there brick or frame apartments, townhouses, or condominiums have been shoehorned into nineteenth-century streetscapes. Oaks, sycamores, maples, and the occasional copper beech tree line quiet streets and shade backyards.

Morris County's 2002 adjusted gross income ranked fifth highest ($95,185) among counties in the nation, with neighboring

Figure 8. Many of Morristown's houses are more than a hundred years old. Some remain single-family homes, others are multifamily buildings, and many have been converted into professional offices.

Somerset ($96,307) and Hunterdon ($94,478) counties fourth and eighth, respectively.[47] Despite Morris County's wealth and resources, Morristown's population is surprisingly diverse. In 2000 whites comprised 67 percent, blacks 17 percent, Asians 4 percent, and Hispanics (of any race) 27 percent. While most of the white and black households have lived in the town for many years, Latinos increased their numbers substantially over the course of the 1990s. Hispanic public school enrollment rose from 8 percent in 1990 to 19 percent in 2000, while white and black enrollments remained relatively stable.[48] Latinos from Mexico, Ecuador, Honduras, and Guatemala, for example, are now heavily concentrated in neighborhoods abutting Morristown's historic African American community. Overcrowding is common and most Latinos live in older frame houses and small apartment buildings. Few are bilingual and many work in low-skilled jobs cleaning houses, washing

Figure 9. Modest Morristown neighborhoods such as this are home to large numbers of Latino immigrants. Long-term residents have complained about housing overcrowding.

cars, caring for lawns, shoveling snow, and building homes. Most have no health-care insurance or other benefits.

The rapid rise in the Latino population brought competition for affordable housing and jobs. Some blacks have voiced concerns that the newcomers bid up the cost of housing when several wage earners crowd a single apartment or house and share the rent. Similarly, charges have been made that Latinos work for lower wages and few, if any, benefits, thus undercutting the employ-ability of some blacks. Although open conflict between Latino and black adults is uncommon, violence among teenagers has ap-peared. For example, in 2003 a small group of African American teens was charged with random street attacks on Latino youths, and two stabbings involving black and Hispanic youths occurred at a local high school. Similar attacks have occurred in a few other North Jersey towns.[49]

While Latinos and African Americans have had their differ-ences, these have largely been neighborhood issues. In the downtown, however, Latinos and the white-dominated business community have clashed. Having struggled for years when the town's economic health was marginal, town merchants and public officials are ever alert to anything threatening business. Over the past decade Latino men have gathered along a main downtown commuter street as early as 6:30 a.m. to seek work for the day. Employers drive up in trucks, vans, and SUVs, negotiate with workers about the terms of the job, and take them directly to the job site. They value Latinos for their cooperative manner, moderate wage demands, and strong work ethic. Employers usually pay workers in cash and few are thought to withhold taxes, Medicare, or Social Security. Occasionally, unscrupulous employers underpay because they know workers are unlikely to complain to police. In other cases, misunderstandings occur owing to language and cultural differences. A substantial number of Latinos are undocumented aliens, although the exact proportion is unknown. Many send part of their earnings to families in Central America.

Police report complaints from merchants and residents that day workers crowd sidewalks, litter, and frighten shoppers. Town officials and Latino advocacy groups have unsuccessfully searched for an alternative day laborer mustering site, but some council members have opposed spending taxpayers' funds for such a purpose.[50] In early 2005 police began a stepped-up campaign against day laborers and employers to enforce state and local laws, motivating advocacy organizations to threaten a lawsuit.[51]

Morristown's leaders are aware that a town-sponsored mustering site in Freehold, New Jersey was closed because it drew even larger numbers of Latino day workers and raised more citizen complaints.[52] Other Greater New York communities, including Plainfield and Somerville, both in North Jersey, have also struggled with the day worker problem. Moreover, Farmingville, New York, a Long Island community, illustrated how friction between residents and Latinos can erupt into violence. In August 2003

Figure 10. Latino immigrants await day jobs along a busy Morristown street. Appearing as early as 6 A.M. five to seven days per week, they triggered complaints from merchants who seek an alternative mustering site outside the business district.

local police arrested four teenagers for allegedly setting fire to a house from which the inhabitants, all Mexicans, escaped. Three years earlier, two Mexican workers were beaten nearly to death by two local men masquerading as employers.[53] Aware of such events, Morristown One Community, a nonprofit organization, and town officials have made efforts to resolve conflicts among competing groups in the town.

While the downtown economy is generally sound, merchants and town officials strive to attract patrons in the face of competition from outlying big box stores and shopping malls. The town's planning strategy seeks to build several hundred apartments and condominiums on lots scattered about the downtown. Boosters hope to attract young singles, childless couples and retirees to live in town and patronize the business community.

Another strategy seeks to increase restaurant and night-life activity on a busy street lying only a few blocks from the historic

Figure 11. Speedwell Avenue is the social and economic center of Morristown's Latino community. Plans to revitalize the corridor have raised fears about harming the town's largest ethnic enclave.

Green. But it, too, has brought contention from the Latino community. The proposed redevelopment area is at the heart of the Latino business district, a three-block strip of restaurants and takeout shops about two blocks from the Green. The development is intended to remedy a dangerous traffic bottleneck by demolishing several older buildings, some containing Latino businesses. Community leaders have protested that Morristown's redevelopment strategy would bring expansion of the commercial sector while destroying the center of the Latino community. Latino businesses would be relocated during construction and their merchants fear increased rents in the new buildings.

Further inflaming tensions, however, was the discovery that a third-generation family-owned business in the project area, originally slated for demolition, was later exempted. Critics suspected favoritism because the business is owned by a non-Latino with allegedly close ties to downtown merchants and town officials.

CHAPTER 3

Not long after, a mysterious fire destroyed the shop and the owner relocated the business to a nearby building. Arson was suspected, but no one was charged with a crime. Attempting to ease tensions, town planning officials have opened a dialogue with Latino and other leaders, most of whom have called for a plan that preserves the multicultural character of the Latino center.

Although contention among whites, African Americans, and Latinos is of concern to community leaders, Morristown's location in the midst of post-suburban North Jersey raises another issue. Two of the eleven New Jersey edge cities identified by Joel Garreau in the early 1990s lie a short drive from Morristown along I-287.[54] Parsippany-Troy Hills and the Bridgewater Mall area are, respectively, north and south of the town.[55] Together with several corporate complexes located on the perimeter of Morristown, these edge cities employ hundreds of residents from Morristown and adjacent communities.[56] Indeed, between 1990 and 2000 the Parsippany-Troy Hills edge city added nearly 11,000 new jobs.[57]

Corporate executives abound in Morris County's leafy suburbs, but many edge-city workers are young singles who live in or near Morristown in one of several condominium or apartment complexes. Most live by themselves or cohabit with a partner or spouse and work in the pharmaceutical, information technology, or biotechnology industries or in finance, insurance or real estate. Some visit Morristown's bars or dance clubs or make occasional visits to Manhattan or Hoboken for a night out. But few appear to have much contact with North Jersey's old cities such as Newark and Elizabeth. Many spend long hours working or commuting by car, and their lives seem to revolve largely between home, job, and weekend recreation. Although their contributions to the town's tax base are significant, few appear to attend public meetings or follow local affairs. Together with black and Latino populations, which tend to have relatively little involvement in town affairs, many young adults have largely relinquished civic involvement to an older generation of long-term, mostly white, residents. In this regard they constitute a faceless citizenry. From the point of view of town officials, the young post-suburbanites may be considered "dream constituents." Through their taxes and patronage of businesses, they help balance the municipal budget, but they ask little, if anything, in return. And although their tendency not to vote in local elections means that they do politicians little good, they do them little harm either.

CONCLUSION

Thus far, this portrait has portrayed North Jersey as a subregion of Greater New York shaped by external and internal forces. The bi-state brokerage of power, proceeding through both cooperation and contention, affects many aspects of life in the Manhattan-North Jersey axis. Internally, the effects of high population density, extraordinary social diversity, drastically shrinking land and natural resources, and seemingly irresolvable conflicts between growth and preservation further challenge the citizens of North Jersey. Experiences in communities such as Montclair and Morristown illustrate some of these conflicts. The next two chapters return to the Manhattan-North Jersey axis to examine matters of identity and image.

Diluting Our Identity

Who are North Jerseyans? Two institutions, both dominated by New York City based industries, shed light on the complications of indigenous identity among North Jerseyans. These are the mass media and professional sports. Unlike the Port Authority, neither of these industries are susceptible to bi-state cooperation through public or civic channels. Instead, the mass media and professional sports, while not untouched by regional geopolitics, respond primarily to the market dynamics of cross-Hudson supply and demand. Together, they contribute in subtle ways to the erosion of sub-regional identity in North Jersey.

NOW THIS: GOTHAM-CENTRIC TELEVISION

Visit nearly any metropolitan area in the United States and tune in the early evening local television news broadcast. From Tucson to Boston, from Miami to Seattle, viewers usually find some or all of the local affiliate broadcasting stations of the four national networks—ABC, NBC, CBS, and Fox. The local affiliates contribute significantly to shaping public perceptions about people and events in their respective metropolitan areas. Indeed, network formats such as "MetroNews" or "Action News" are a standard fixture in all of the larger metropolitan areas of the nation.

This pattern is apparent in Greater New York as well. WABC, WNBC, WCBS, and WNYW (Fox), all located in Manhattan, provide morning, evening, and nighttime area news broadcasts. Like other metropolitan area local affiliates, these stations seem to emphasize the long-held credo in television broadcasting, "If it bleeds, it leads." Typically, their half-hour local news programs feature reportage about dramatic events such as fires, accidents, crimes, labor strikes, and political demonstrations.[1] New Jersey viewers seem to be aware of this pattern. A 1999 survey revealed that 70 percent of registered voters thought that television news coverage of violence was aimed primarily at drawing more viewers and enhancing ratings, rather than at providing news that people "need to know." Fifty-eight percent thought that television coverage gave too much attention to violent crimes, while 36 percent thought that it gave about the right amount.[2]

Attention to dramatic events, in addition to the sports, weather, traffic, and commercials, plus periodic consumer news, personal health information, and human interest stories, round out the typical news broadcasts. Attention to government and civic affairs is generally centered on New York City. Such matters in the suburban towns and state capitals of New Jersey and Connecticut generally receive a lower priority.[3]

Further compromising local news coverage, however is New York's identity as a global city. Like Washington, D.C., it is a daily setting for national and international news events. When heads of state visit Manhattan, when key events unfold at the United Nations, when Wall Street financial tremors occur, the network affiliates often preempt local news programming to report on them. For millions of Greater New York viewers living in suburban areas such as North Jersey, the unique status of the Gotham-centered network affiliates means that coverage of local and state government, and political, cultural, and economic news often receives short shrift.

Another factor diluting area local news coverage is the sheer size of the broadcast region. There are more than 1,600 government units and 21 million residents in the Greater New York broadcast market. Understandably, systematic coverage of state, regional, and local news in the tri-state area is impossible in a half-hour nightly news show. A study of local evening newscasts on New York City's WABC, WCBS, and WNBC television stations during New Jersey's November 4, 2001 elections highlights the problem. It found that a total of 489 minutes of campaign news coverage was collectively devoted to the New York mayoralty and New Jersey gubernatorial campaigns over the thirty days preceding the elections. Of this amount, however, only 86 minutes (17.6 percent) was spent on the New Jersey race. Although New Jersey residents compose approximately 30 percent of all viewers in the New York area, their governor's race received less than 20 percent of the total time allocated to election coverage among the three affiliates.[4] Because the local affiliates tend to increase the air time devoted to covering "big" political events such as statewide election campaigns, lower profile matters such as municipal and state legislative elections fade into the background.

The dilemma of inadequate local and state news coverage has plagued North Jersey for decades. In the late 1970s, for example, Harrison Williams, then a Democratic U.S. Senator from New Jersey, wrote of New York's and Philadelphia's dominance in local television coverage. He portrayed the state as "merely the supporting actor in the shadow of two great cities to the north and south."[5] Other observers were even more candid. One railed against "the prevalence of externally based metropolitan news media whose writers and commentators apparently attempt to gain reputations as sophisticates by sneering at the suburbs, particularly New Jersey."[6] Referring to New York City and Philadelphia, another critic noted that "the majority of the state's residents tend to identify more with their respective metropolitan areas than with the state as an entity."[7] A third observer noted that the lack of a "clear and positive state self-identity" has persisted since colonial times, and that the increasingly bipolarized pattern of growth in the Philadelphia and New York regions has worsened the problem.[8]

Why haven't any of the national broadcast networks opened a station in New Jersey? Whatever their interest in doing so, the Federal Communications Commission has refused to issue a license permitting it. Although in 2000 the Garden State had the ninth largest state population nationally, its small land area squeezes its broadcast market between the "bookends" of Philadelphia and New York City.[9] Local affiliates in these two cities thus divide the Jersey population into two sub-groups.[10] As a result, viewers in North Jersey tend to turn to the New York affiliates for local news, while those in South Jersey tend to turn to the Philadelphia affiliates. Still, it would be unfair to suggest that a New York City orientation in local news coverage has been "forced" on North Jersey viewers. In fact, for decades North Jerseyans have had the option of watching news on their state's own public television channel.

New Jersey Network (NJN) traces its origins to the early 1960s. Public officials in New Jersey had become frustrated over the tendency of New York broadcasters to give short shrift to New Jersey's affairs. In response, the state legislature established the state's own public television channel. Each weekday, NJN broadcasts several hours of state and local news coverage, with emphasis on governmental, political, civic, business, and environmental issues. By most measures, it seems, the Emmy Award winning NJN has filled the gap in news coverage, especially for North Jersey and the state's capital, Trenton. It downplays accidents, fires, and similar dramatic events, and features stories emanating from its primary funding sources, state government, major in-state corporations, and foundations. For example, 42 percent of NJN's

2004 budget of nearly $17.7 million was funded from state sources.[11] But being heavily state-funded, NJN has not fully succeeded in projecting the independent stature some viewers would like. Perhaps in response, entrepreneurs formed News12, a commercial channel, in the late 1990s. It provides extensive daily coverage of local and state news, especially of events in the state capital and in North Jersey (where its broadcast facilities are located). Between NJN and News12, then, coverage of New Jersey public affairs has improved significantly.

But there are signs that these stations reach relatively small numbers of North Jersey's viewers. For example, according to one source, about 107,000 of New Jersey's approximately 3 million households watch *NJN News*, the station's signature program. By comparison, New York's network affiliates attract about five times as many viewers from New Jersey. [12] While ample local news programming is available to North Jerseyans, apparently, far more of them are receptive to a New York-based orientation of public affairs.[13] Then there is the case of Greater New York's highly diverse and competitive newspaper market.

READ ALL ABOUT IT: A FRAGMENTED NEWSPAPER LANDSCAPE

In most American metropolises, one or two newspapers dominate area readership. The *Globe* and the *Herald* in Boston, the *Times-Picayune* in New Orleans, the *American-Statesman* in Austin— each illustrates the influence of long-established print journalism organizations on metropolitan life. Like local television news broadcasts, each newspaper helps to shape people's perspectives about public life regionally and statewide. There is no question that a few North Jersey newspapers such as the *Star-Ledger*, *The Record*, and the *Jersey Journal* outpace their competitors in local and state news coverage.[14] Of these, the *Star-Ledger*, headquartered in Newark, has the largest daily circulation at more than 400,000.[15] Yet, the circulations of four New York newspapers vastly exceed this: the *Wall Street Journal* (1.8 million), the *New York Times* (1.1 million), the *Daily News* (715,000), and the *New York Post* (590,000). In addition, *USA Today*, a nationally oriented publication, has a circulation in excess of 2.1 million.[16] They all compete actively for readers in Greater New York, while the *Star-Ledger* is confined largely to a North Jersey audience. In addition to more specialized publications such as the *Financial Times*, these newspapers are distributed via home delivery or at street kiosks and vending machines throughout the region. Yet, a second source of competition comes from many foreign language newspapers, especially those in Spanish or Asian languages, which are targeted to immigrant communities. These publications tend to carry little, if any, news about social, economic, cultural, or political matters in North Jersey. Consequently, their North Jersey readers may be better informed about events and issues in other parts of the world than about those in their own civic backyard.

A 2003 survey examining New Jerseyans' knowledge of the partisan identity of state officials measured the severity of the problem. The poll discovered that while most New Jerseyans could correctly answer one or two of the following questions, only 4 percent could answer all three:

1. Which party does the majority of members of the state assembly belong to?
2. Which party does the majority of members of the state senate belong to?
3. What is the governor's political party affiliation?

The poll director observed that New Jerseyans were "pretty much clueless about the balance of power in Trenton."[17] The findings

were especially noteworthy because the partisan identity of legislative and gubernatorial politicians is so routinely indicated in
daily news coverage. Another New Jersey survey in the same year
pointed out that one-third of those polled could not identify the
state's then-governor.[18] Another survey revealed that 87 percent
of New Jersey respondents did not know what state offices were
included in the November 2003 elections.[19]

Furthermore, the same study found that television news viewers were less knowledgeable about these matters than newspaper readers. It acknowledged that the "age-old problem of
television in New Jersey" resulted in most local news coming from
out-of-state broadcasters, leaving those who claimed to get their
news from television no more knowledgeable about state political
matters than those who said they don't watch television.[20] Perhaps it is no surprise then, that less than one-half of those surveyed (43 percent) indicated that they follow news about politics
and government "regularly."[21]

These results describe New Jerseyans statewide, rather than
simply those living in North Jersey. If anything, however, there is
reason to believe that many North Jerseyans are even less knowledgeable about in-state public affairs than other Jerseyans. This
is due to the stronger historical ties in North Jersey to New York
City's events and institutions. Similarly, many people in South
and Central Jersey pay closer attention to Philadelphia's current
affairs.

Certainly, similar dynamics appear in other metropolitan
areas, especially the larger ones. But few people in those places
are likely to contend with the range and diversity of media
choices that exist in Greater New York. Nor are they as likely to
experience the sheer attention-getting magnetism of a global city
such as New York, with its diversity of cultural, diplomatic, publishing, advertising, and business institutions. Doubtless, some

North Jerseyans live where they do in order to partake of these attractions. But doing so poses additional challenges to the formation and maintenance of subregional civic identity.

The apparently widely varying contours of public interest in civic matters in North Jersey have several explanations. Many inhabitants are *former* residents of New York City who moved to the North Jersey suburbs to raise families.[22] Many of these people could be expected to maintain their interest in New York affairs and have less concern for New Jersey matters. Similarly, former inhabitants of other nations often follow events in their native land more closely than New Jersey's affairs.[23] Still others are "snowbirds" who spend part of each year in Florida or other sunny places.[24] Thus, while New Jerseyans are more likely to get their information about state affairs from newspapers than from television, the newspaper market in North Jersey is highly diverse, polyglot and dispersed.[25] Public attention to local civic matters is thus fragmented. For these and other reasons cities such as Newark, Paterson, Elizabeth and Jersey City have a particularly difficult time focusing public attention on social and economic issues.

For many North Jerseyans, Manhattan is the *only* true downtown, the supreme locus of civic and cultural life. For these citizens, the civic center of North Jersey is on the east, not the west, side of the Hudson River. And the powerful reach of the Gotham-based media helps to nurture and perpetuate this pattern. One North Jerseyan rhapsodized about working in, relaxing in, and attending college in New York City, describing people such as himself as "de facto New York City residents."[26] Furthermore, he observed, "Because of our nearness, we are still an integral part of it, whether we want to be or not. We are still under New York City's umbrella—its mode of living, its economics and virtually all else."[27]

This is not to suggest that all, or even most, North Jerseyans have eyes only for Manhattan. Some residents follow local events in North Jersey more closely. But the powerful pull of outside news sources and the highly balkanized pattern of local governments do much to water down individual identity with the subregion or the state.

SPORTS FANS AND ABSENTEE TEAMS

Professional sports, especially with regard to major league teams in baseball, basketball, football and hockey, constitute another industry with similar effects. In Greater New York there are eight such teams.[28] Professional sports teams are usually associated with local pride and place identity. This is because most teams play their games in or near a central city, drawing the bulk of their fans from the surrounding metropolitan area. The teams are usually named after their home city. But once again, the situation in Greater New York is not as simple.

In North Jersey, as in other parts of Greater New York, place identity in major league sports tends to center on New York City. Six of the eight professional teams call Gotham their home, while the remaining two are headquartered in North Jersey (Map 5, p. 88). Ironically, New Jersey is among the most heavily populated states in the nation. Yet, among them, it is the only state to have as few as two major league sports teams. Michigan, Ohio, Florida, and Illinois, for example, have as many as three or four teams in a single large city such as Chicago or Detroit. And even though states such as Arizona, Colorado, Georgia, Wisconsin, and Missouri each had fewer residents in 2000 than the Garden State, they each had more major league teams.

If this were not puzzling enough, as of 2005 New Jersey was scheduled to lose one of its two teams, the New Jersey Nets of the National Basketball Association. The Nets and the New Jersey Devils of the National Hockey League currently play home games

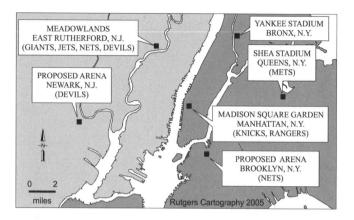

Map 5. Existing and proposed professional sports facilities in New York City and North Jersey demonstrate the bi-state nature of major league sports in Greater New York and represent another venue for conflict spanning the Hudson.

in North Jersey. However, the owner of the Nets plans to relocate his team to New York City's Brooklyn borough, where he has signed an agreement to build a new arena.[29] Considering that average household income in New Jersey is among the highest nationally, some observers are baffled by the paucity of major league teams in the state.

Part of the explanation for this puzzle is that the major league empires in New York City and Philadelphia, much like their mass media empires, tend to dominate New Jersey. In doing so, they serve as absentee purveyors of professional sports to Garden State fans, dividing them into two subregional markets. South Jerseyans tend to follow the Philadelphia teams: the Phillies in baseball, the Eagles in football, the 76ers in basketball, and the Flyers in hockey. North Jerseyans, in contrast, are more likely to be fans of the New York-based teams: the Yankees and Mets in baseball, the Giants and Jets in football, the Knickerbockers in basketball, and the Rangers in hockey. Once again, the dominance of the bipolar metropolitan pattern created by New York City and Philadelphia divides New Jersey residents by subregion.

It is not easy to be a professional sports fan in North Jersey. To attend Yankees home games, for example, residents have to drive a car, often in rush-hour traffic, or take a train to Manhattan, followed by a mass transit trip to the stadium in the Bronx. (Mets home games in Queens are even more distant.) Knicks and Rangers games are more accessible to Jerseyans, but they require driving a car or taking the train to Manhattan's Madison Square Garden. In the years following 1976, when the state-owned Meadowlands Sports Complex opened, North Jerseyans were finally able to attend professional football, basketball, and hockey events on Jersey soil. Located in the tiny town of East Rutherford, the complex is just a few minutes' drive north of Newark.[30] The New York Giants and the New York Jets play home games at Giants Stadium, which is accessible by car or express bus.[31] North Jersey football fans have an advantage over North Jersey baseball fans because their teams play on home ground. But, like them, they are still in the unenviable position of rooting for teams that bear "New York," not "New Jersey," in their names. Although many North Jerseyans are avid Giants or Jets fans, the teams do little to enhance residents' place identity.

Nevertheless, if North Jersey professional baseball and football fans are deprived of home-state pride, professional basketball and hockey fans command less sympathy. The Devils and the Nets not only bear the state name, they play their home games at North Jersey's Meadowlands Sports Complex. Until the mid-1990s though, neither team had propelled New Jersey into championship circles. Then, in the 1995–96 season the Devils began to win hockey games—lots of them—and were crowned the Stanley Cup champions. Proving that their prowess was not a fluke, the team repeated its feat in 1999–2000.[32] Perhaps inspired by the Devils, the Nets surprised everyone in 2002 by winning the NBA Eastern Conference title, only to lose the national title to the Los Angeles Lakers.[33] And, for the third time in their short life as a team, the

Devils won the Stanley Cup, this time in 2002 against the Anaheim Mighty Ducks. The following year the Nets repeated their success, winning the Eastern Conference title but losing the national championship to the San Antonio Spurs. By any reasonable measure, these two teams, whose fan bases are largely in North Jersey, had done much to expand the state's modest profile in major league sports.

One would think that these sports triumphs would create long lines at ticket offices. And indeed, the sale of tickets, concessions, and sports paraphernalia rose somewhat during the Nets' and Devils' home playoff and championship games. Yet they lagged well behind figures for many other NBA and NHL teams.[34] The many empty seats at home games told the story: even with nationally ranked New Jersey teams, North Jersey fans were not turning out in numbers considered even average in other metropolitan areas.

Professional sports thus pose an odd picture in North Jersey. Basketball and hockey fans can watch in-state teams play their home games on North Jersey soil. Football enthusiasts, in contrast, watch out-of-state teams play home games on Garden State turf. Those who enjoy baseball are at the bottom of the pecking order because there are no in-state or out-of-state major league teams playing in New Jersey. Baseball fans must travel to Queens or the Bronx to watch the Mets and the Yankees, respectively. Sports pundits and team officials have pondered the reasons for uneven support for professional sports among North Jerseyans. Some note that North Jersey basketball fans are split between those who follow the Nets and those who follow the New York Knicks; correspondingly, hockey fans are divided by those who root for the Devils and those who cheer for the New York Rangers. Because the New York team franchises are much older than those in New Jersey, many North Jerseyans have followed them since childhood.[35] Other fans are former New York City residents whose allegiances have not flagged. Old habits die hard, and thus not all North Jersey basketball and hockey enthusiasts are moved to support New Jersey teams.

Another explanation for tepid team support is the isolated location of the Meadowlands complex and accessibility issues for many residents.[36] But the problem here may be in the nature of urbanism and population distribution in the state. As noted above, New Jersey has no real central city of dominance within its borders. For many North Jerseyans, New York City has served that purpose. Neither Newark, Jersey City, Elizabeth, or Paterson has the critical mass of population or the cultural, entertainment, or civic attractions to serve as the focal center of a large metropolitan area. North Jersey's pattern of crustal urbanization, discussed earlier, has dispersed the potential fan base over a relatively large, undifferentiated multicounty area. This creates problems of fan accessibility to each of these cities while also inhibiting the formation of a single civic center for expressions of subregional pride and collective enterprise.

Indeed, this matter was highlighted when the Nets and the Devils celebrated their recent title victories—not with traditional, downtown, ticker-tape parades, but instead with tailgate parties in the Meadowlands parking lot.[37] In concert with North Jersey's pattern of granulated local government and the tendency of many class, ethnic, racial, and religious groups to live in tightly knit enclaves, the subregion's lack of a true urban center tends to discourage large-scale, collective expressions of group solidarity.[38] Like North Jersey's atypical mass-media landscape, its atypical professional sports setting has done little to advance subregional identity. Perhaps, then, it was only a matter of time before the momentum would develop to bring major league sports to New Jersey's largest city, Newark.

NEWARK, A HIGHLY CHALLENGED CITY

Located but a seventeen-mile drive west of New York City, Newark in 2000 was composed of 14 percent non-Hispanic whites, 53 percent non-Hispanic blacks, and 30 percent Hispanics (of both races).[39] It is one of the most severely challenged American cities, with among the highest rates of unemployment, poverty, school dropouts, and other measures of social distress in New Jersey.[40] One of the nation's most tragic civil disturbances in the late 1960s contributed to the city's struggles to overcome tremendous losses in housing, retail shops, employment, and tax revenues. Many thousands of people, mainly whites, moved out of the city after the 1967 violence, and the population declined from 405,000 in 1960 to 273,000 in 2000.[41] Like other cities, Newark was further devastated by the closing or downsizing of factories and related businesses, which accelerated over the course of the 1980s and 1990s. Although it remains the largest employment center in New Jersey, it lost approximately five thousand jobs throughout the 1990s.[42] The downtown retail center struggles with crime and a shabby appearance. The city is flanked by the communities of East Orange, Orange, and Irvington, all of which have gained large numbers of poor and working-class minorities over the past three decades. Located in Essex County, these four communities stand in sharp relief to other towns around them. Their crime, poverty, and unemployment rates far exceed those of other Essex communities, and abandoned or poorly maintained properties infest several neighborhoods. Although federally subsidized clearance of public housing projects has created opportunities for neighborhood renewal, neighbors complain about long delays in rebuilding on these sites. Newark, with the largest number of poor households in the state, receives substantial federal and state aid. In 1995 the state government took control of the city's

Figure 12. Demolition in 2005 erased the long-defunct Pabst brewery, which had been emblematic of the city's industrial decline. The bottle-shaped tank, visible for miles around, was once Newark's most identifiable landmark.

public school system, owing to financial and other irregularities and poorly performing students. Moreover, crime has long been a major issue. In 2004, for example, 365 people were wounded and 68 were killed by guns.[43]

Despite these hard realities, Newark has made important

Figure 13. Abandoned or poorly maintained private units such as this are scattered over wide areas of Newark. Rehabilitation is no longer feasible for many.

Figure 14. Lively Market Street is at the center of Newark's retail downtown. Police maintain a regular presence in response to fears about crime.

strides on the "rough road to renaissance."[44] For example, a state supreme court decision resulted in more than $5 billion being earmarked for thirty distressed school districts, including Newark's, to pay for new schools and preschool programs. The newly built New Jersey Performing Arts Center opened in downtown Newark in 1997, followed shortly by a minor league baseball stadium for the Newark Bears.[45]A handsome art deco office tower was restored and has become a premier downtown address. Recently, the Federal Bureau of Investigation occupied a new office tower. Fiber optic cable was installed throughout the downtown and the city's first Internet "hotel" opened in a former department store. Major employers such as Prudential Financial Services, Public Service Electric and Gas, and Horizon Blue Cross Blue Shield have remained in the downtown, and newer corporations such as MBNA and IDT have opened offices. Five institutions of higher education and three hospitals are located in the city.

For more than three decades African Americans have enjoyed significant power in the city's political system. Sharpe James, the city's second African American mayor, was first elected in 1986. Minorities are heavily represented on city, county, school district, and housing authority payrolls. The city council is dominated by blacks, but a growing Latino population has increased Latino representation. Mistrust between some African American and Latino politicians has discouraged consistent alliances and common goals.

Newark's largest employers have increased minority employment in recent decades. But these firms are dominated by white board members, executives, and managers, the vast majority of whom live in the suburbs. Blacks play a larger role in the civic community, albeit many of its organizations depend heavily for their support on these corporations as well as on the state government and foundations. Consequently, while cooperation among whites, blacks, and Latinos in corporate, civic, and politi-

Figure 15. The long-heralded Newark "renaissance" proceeds in fits and starts. A dedicated booster, Prudential Financial Services (right) has spent millions of dollars to advance the city's comeback.

Figure 16. The New Jersey Performing Arts Center, opened in 1997, is often referred to as the "jewel in the crown" of Newark.

Figure 17. In several Newark neighborhoods infill housing such as these units has been built. The city often offers subsidies such as discounts on land prices and tax concessions.

cal realms is not unusual, the underlying tensions are evident to observers. Various attempts to forge public-private alliances between city hall and members of the business community have surfaced over the years, but the distrust on both sides is always apparent and sometimes palpable. Doubtless, the city's greatest assets are the many talented people and organizations that have labored tirelessly through good times and bad on behalf of Newark's worthy civic and social causes.

Divisions within and between the business and political communities are further exacerbated by tensions between city hall and the middle- and upper-income suburban towns of Essex County. Mistrust runs deep on both sides and many Newark residents remember when whites abandoned the city en mass throughout the 1960s and 1970s. Some fear that whites will wrest control over city politics through the state government or Newark's business organizations. Meanwhile, suburban whites com-

Figure 18. Mayor Sharpe James has held forth in Newark's classical revival city hall since 1986. A nine-member council poses only a modest counterbalance to his power.

plain about higher county and state taxes, heavy subsidies to Newark's government, and perceived waste, mismanagement, and dishonesty in city hall, the school system, and the housing authority. Caught between the city and suburbs is the Essex County government, like Newark city hall a fortress of Democratic strength. The two groups regularly deliver city and county majority votes to Democratic state house and gubernatorial candidates. Together with Democrats from other New Jersey urban areas, Newark and Essex County often stand as a bulwark against predominantly Republican suburban and rural interests.

NEWARK AND THE ARENA

Since the late 1990s Mayor James has pressed for construction of a professional sports arena in downtown Newark. Like the arts

Figure 19. Newark's hockey arena, to be constructed here, has raised considerable controversy because of city hall's $200+ million subsidy and a relatively small fan base.

center, the facility is intended to draw suburbanites into the city
to spend money and to stimulate development, create jobs, and
increase tax revenues. There have been many twists and turns in
the arena saga but by 2005 plans called for a $310 million project,
including a Devils' hockey rink, a hotel, a conference center, restaurants, and parking. At one time, however, there were grander
aspirations: the original proposal was to include a combination
basketball (Nets) and hockey (Devils) arena and several nearby
facilities. The projected cost was $355 million. But this plan de-
pended on substantial financial support from state and county
sources to subsidize construction. It was boldly introduced to the
public at an invitation-only conference in October 2000 entitled
"The Newark Arena: Benefits for the New Jersey Economy."[46]

With television cameras whirring, James opened the event by
speaking passionately for the project. At one point he began sing-

ing "The Impossible Dream," causing several attendees to shuffle their feet and steal sidelong glances at one another. The mayor added a special stanza endorsing the arena.

Following James, Lewis Katz, then a co-owner of the Nets, echoed the mayor's enraptured prose. In mellifluous tones, he asked the audience to envision the arena's opening night, with crowds streaming forward, spotlights ablaze, a Goodyear Blimp hovering overhead, and cameras televising the event to the nation. The implication was clear: once and for all, the arena would put Newark on the national map and help transform its downcast image. Asked how he thought Newark's youth would respond to the arena, Katz confessed uncertainty, opining that perhaps their "self-esteem" would be enhanced. (Within a few years, perhaps frustrated by delays, Katz would be involved in efforts to move the Nets to Brooklyn.)

Jayson Williams, a former Nets star, also endorsed the project and spoke of its appeal to youths. (Less than four years later Williams would be tried for the 2002 shotgun death of a chauffeur at his exurban New Jersey estate.)[47]

Several more speakers chimed in, including the Essex County Executive. (He would be convicted by the U.S. Attorney's office in 2003 for accepting political contributions in return for county road repair contracts).[48] When presentations were over, reporters and audience members raised questions about arena financing. Team owner Katz, in particular, was pressed for clarification but he tiptoed around specifics. He quoted his mother that, "It's not what it costs, it's what you can get out of it," that matters. Coming to Katz's rescue, the Essex County Executive, one of the most ardent proponents, chided questioners that the discourse had taken an "interesting turn," and implied that critical scrutiny was unwarranted.

Before too long, the city's lone daily newspaper, the *Star-Ledger*, while posing reservations about financing, endorsed the

project on the basis of presumed benefits to Newark.[49] Throughout 2001 questions continued to surface about several aspects of
the arena. For example, the YankeeNets organization, then the
owners of the Nets and the Devils, were displeased with low gate
receipts at both teams' home games. Some board members were
not convinced that moving the teams from the Meadowlands
Sports Complex to Newark would substantially increase atten-
dance.[50] A second concern surfaced from the New Jersey Sports
and Exposition Authority, the state agency that owns the Meadowlands complex. Seeing no benefit in losing the teams to a Newark arena, the Authority launched a counter attack. It pledged
to renovate the Meadowlands arena, improve accessibility, and
permit a developer to build a large family entertainment center
next door.

Competition between the Authority and the city of Newark for
the Nets and Devils was underway. It was clear that, should the
Newark arena be built, it would have to compete with the nearby
Meadowlands facility for other revenue-producing events such as
circuses and rock concerts. Thus, bidding wars between city- and
state-owned arenas would be likely. Further beclouding the Newark arena proposal was the $355 million cost estimate. The price
tag was first set in 2000 and there were concerns that it was too
low. Nationally, projected sports facility expenses are notoriously
underestimated and there were good reasons for concerns about
cost overruns.[51]

Public opinion was another matter. Would sufficient numbers
of visitors come to the Newark arena? Would the arena measur-
ably advance Newark's revitalization? Would it offer significant
numbers of new jobs for Newark's residents and enhance the
city's tax base sufficiently? Several public opinion surveys cast
doubts about citizen support for the arena. Questioning the popularity of the Nets among state residents, a January 1999 statewide
poll indicated that 92 percent of the respondents had not at-

tended a Nets game in the previous year.[52] A second issue concerned the willingness of fans to attend home games in Newark. Another 1999 survey revealed that whites were less enthusiastic than minorities about visiting Newark.[53] As plans for the arena grew more finite, a third poll, in 2002, queried residents of Essex, the county in which Newark is located. Only 5.2 percent of those surveyed said they would visit Newark more frequently if the arena were built.[54] A fourth poll, conducted at about the same time, asked residents statewide at which location they would prefer to attend Nets or Devils games. By a margin of nearly two to one they preferred the Meadowlands arena over a Newark facility.[55] A fifth survey found similarly discouraging results later in 2002; one-third of the state's registered voters preferred moving the Nets and Devils to Newark, while 57 percent opposed it.[56] As the arena issue continued to fulminate, public attitudes became more starkly polarized. Then, in September 2003 yet another survey was completed. Rumors of team owner frustration over delays in building a Newark arena raised questions about how much New Jerseyans valued the Nets. The statewide poll found that most residents thought that professional sports teams are good for the state's economy and boost its image. But if the Nets moved to a different state, nearly one-half would not miss the team, while 20 percent would miss the team "a great deal."[57] By almost any public measure then, the Newark arena was not widely popular in New Jersey or North Jersey. Where support did exist, public preferences leaned toward a privately financed project. These and other negative signs contributed to the governor's decision to remain aloof from the project and pledge only modest state financing.[58]

Thanks to a windfall payment of $265 million pledged to the city of Newark by the Port Authority, Mayor James was able to eliminate the issue of large-scale state financing for the arena.[59] In mid-2002 he announced that Newark would build an arena without heavy state subsidies, contributing $165 million to the arena from its Port Authority revenues, plus $35 million from bond issuances. Under this plan, the YankeeNets would provide an additional $155 million, the state's redevelopment authority $10 million, and other sources $15 million.

However, critics questioned how Newark could spend $200 million on a sports arena and still expect the state to spend upwards of a half-billion dollars to subsidize the city's education and social welfare costs. Also questioned were the opportunity costs of spending the windfall on an arena versus making investments in improving city schools, health, employment, neighborhood revitalization, and other social needs.[60] Soon a citizen lawsuit was filed to prevent the city from spending the $200 million on an arena. Mayor James called the action "irresponsible behavior and political posturing" and said that the arena offered "enormous promise" for Newark. When asked why the city failed to seek public opinions about funding the arena, James replied, "We are the public."[61] Still, while some people approved of the arena proposal, negative opinions seemed to predominate.[62]

After several years of controversy concerning Newark's arena it was announced in early 2004 that the Nets would be sold to a new owner, who planned to move the team in 2009 from the Meadowlands Sports Complex to Brooklyn. New York's city hall pledged millions of dollars in subsidies to build an arena for the team.[63] Regardless of their views about the Nets or the arena, North Jerseyans could not miss the underlying message that, in a contest involving money, once again the Big Apple ruled.

Obsessed with leaving Newark the legacy of an arena, Mayor James pushed on. Within a month he announced that the city would build an eighteen-thousand-seat Devils hockey arena at a cost of $300 million, with the city increasing its contribution to $210 million and the team paying for the remainder.[64] To open in 2007, the facility would be accompanied by a three-hundred-room hotel, eight office buildings, retail space, and a parking structure.

Once again, though, a proposal for a Newark arena was plagued by doubts.[65]

A day after the mayor's announcement, a study was released showing that the National Hockey League had a collective operating loss of $273 million in the 2002–2003 season.[66] Owners of the Devils acknowledged a team debt of $70 million in early 2004.[67] To some observers, it appeared that the Devils were looking to Newark and the new arena to rescue the team from an ocean of red ink. The problem with this reasoning is that Newark, unlike cities such as Boston, Milwaukee, Minneapolis-St. Paul, Toronto, or Montreal, has never been a hotbed of hockey hoopla. Without a hometown base of fans, the Devils will have to attract droves of followers from the suburbs simply to break even. And the arena will have to compete with the Meadowlands and other area venues for income from non-Devils events such as rock concerts. Regardless of city hall's "build-it-and-they-will-come" mentality, these prospects have left many observers in doubt about the arena's viability.

METS, NETS, JETS . . . NUTS!

While Newark spent years trying to hitch its wagon to an arena star, other events portray the hotly contested atmosphere of professional sports in Greater New York. In early 2004 New York City proposed bringing the Jets home to Gotham by building a new stadium directly across the Hudson River on the west side of Manhattan. Mayor Michael Bloomberg insisted that the stadium was a public necessity if the city was to compete successfully for the 2012 Olympic Games. By mid-2005 both ventures had collapsed. By the end of 2005 plans were announced to build a new stadium at the Meadowlands for the Giants and the Jets.[68]

Bi-state contention over professional sports is nothing new in Greater New York. In the 1970s New Jersey built the Meadowlands

Sports Complex and lured the Giants and Jets to play their home games at the facility. The *New York Times* launched an editorial assault, accusing New Jersey of forsaking regional interests.[69] Occurring in the wake of New York City's catastrophic fiscal crisis, the event signaled another turn for the worse at a time when Gothamites desperately needed to recover their once-vaunted image. Thus, the latest trans-Hudson dispute over the two football teams only continues a long-standing rivalry.

Thus, similar to several other metropolitan areas, business and political leaders in Greater New York (and especially, those in the Manhattan-North Jersey axis) contest for professional sports visibility. They do so, in part, based on the assumption that major league teams bring major league identity to cities and states. Whatever the risks to New York City in this strategy, the risks to Newark and North Jersey are far greater. Implicit is the reality that teams gain as much, if not more, by association with the New York name as the city gains by having them. In North Jersey, however, some leaders hope to gain far more from association with the Devils (the only true New Jersey major league team) than the team is likely to deliver. Given the team's shaky financial condition, weak public interest in hockey, and excessive subsidies to the team from a financially strapped city, there is much to worry about in the years ahead.

CHAPTER FIVE

Harming Our Image

If factors such as poor local news coverage and externally dominated professional sports franchises do much to weaken North
Jersey's identity, other conditions actively undermine perceptions
of the subregion's public safety and governmental integrity. Organized crime and political corruption have been especially prominent. Together, these realities help to shape an image of the
character and quality of life in the Garden State, and especially in
its northern half, that collectively erodes its reputation.[1]

In one respect it is a paradox that Jerseyans struggle with identity and image, given the state's many attributes. It has bountiful
historical sites, major corporate employers, many attractive communities, one of the best commuter rail systems in the nation,
the scenic Highlands region, popular Atlantic beaches, and a level
of cultural diversity in its population matched by few, if any, U.S.
metropolitan areas. And yet, although Garden State households
have among the highest average incomes and the most highly
educated populations nationally, the issue of image has troubled
some North Jerseyans for a very long time.[2] Among the dimensions of image are public perceptions of official graft and mob
racketeering.

NEW YORK, PHILADELPHIA, AND THE MAFIA

Indigenous gangs of street toughs have been a part of North Jersey's urban centers at least since the late nineteenth century. As long ago as 1927 the gangster Abner "Longy" Zwillman, already North Jersey's gambling and bootlegging czar, formed a partnership with the New York mob chieftain Charles "Lucky" Luciano and his followers. Soon, they opened a string of gambling casinos, primarily in Bergen and Hudson counties, both of which are easily reached from Manhattan. The opening of the George Washington Bridge and the Lincoln and Holland tunnels over the late 1920s and 1930s permitted New York mobsters, much like legitimate businesses, to expand their markets to the Jersey suburbs. While Philadelphia mobsters set up gambling, prostitution and loansharking enterprises in parts of South Jersey and the Jersey shore, North Jersey became the center of racketeering activity in the Garden State, resulting in no small measure from the subregion's proximity to New York City.[3]

With time, North Jersey became integrated into the territories of several Manhattan-based gangster organizations. Known collectively over the years as the Mafia, the Cosa Nostra, the Syndicate, or the Mob, their members formed a vertically-integrated command structure beginning in the late 1920s under the joint authority of five organized crime "families" in New York City.[4] A commission, made up of representatives of the major organized crime gangs in the nation, was formed, with Zwillman representing North Jersey rackets. The commission divided America's major urban crime markets into zones and assigned exclusive franchise over the rackets to individual gangs. Policies to reduce competition and resolve conflicts between gangs were adopted by the commission.[5] Even after the repeal of Prohibition, the New York and North Jersey mobsters generally prospered throughout the 1930s, 1940s and 1950s.[6]

However, increasing pressure from the press and law enforcement agencies began to whittle away at mob activities. Televised U.S. Senate committee hearings on organized crime in 1950 and 1951 placed the problem in the national public eye, feeding growing concerns in New York and New Jersey about negative public images.[7] Zwillman, who was forced to testify during these proceedings, was found dead in his home in 1959, allegedly a suicide victim. Although other North Jersey crime bosses would emerge in the years ahead, none would ever achieve the stature of Zwillman with the New York crime syndicate.[8] Consequently, the Genovese, Gambino, Columbo, Bonanno, and Lucchese crime families of New York gradually took control of many of the most lucrative North Jersey rackets. Once again, North Jersey suffered under Gotham-based colonial rule, this time by a beefy *capo de capo* and his *consigliere*, rather than by a bewigged royal governor and his sheriffs.

But increasing public displeasure with racketeering propelled federal and state agencies to crack down. As North Jersey's suburban business and political leaders sought to attract New York's firms and families to relocate, they strove to sanitize the subregion's image. This would be difficult to do with such gangland figures in the news as Anthony "Little Pussy" Russo, Pasquale "Patty Mack" Macchiarole, Emilio "The Count" Delio, Joseph Arthur "Bayonne Joe" Zicarelli, Alphonse "Funzi" Tieri, and John "Johnny Coca Cola" Lardiere (aka Larducci).[9] So in the 1970s the Garden State began in earnest to prune its gangland weeds.

Despite state and federal efforts, however, by the 1980s New Jersey was termed "a state infested with organized crime."[10] The Lucchese family, in particular, carried on "illegal gambling, loansharking, narcotics trafficking, and the takeover of legitimate businesses."[11] But by the mid-1990s the growing success of wiretapping and laws such as the federal RICO statutes helped to cripple severely several mob enterprises in North and Central Jersey. Leading the charge were the F.B.I and the U.S. Attorney's Office in Newark, which succeeded in convicting alleged Lucchese crime family members Michael and Martin Tacetta and Michael Perna.[12] Genovese family members, Tino Fiumara, Raymond Tango, and Giacomo "Jackie" DiNorscio were also imprisoned, as were the Gambino family boss, Samuel "Little Sammy" Corsaro and his associate, Anthony "Tony Pro" Proto.[13]

THE RACKETS

Over the years North Jersey organized crime units have run a variety of illegal enterprises. Gambling, loansharking, prostitution, drug dealing, compulsory protection, hijacking, and labor union embezzlement are among the most common. For example, in 2003 New Jersey's State Police secured loansharking indictments against seventeen men, including Ludwig "Ninny" Bruschi of Jackson, N.J., a caporegime or captain of New Jersey operations for the Genovese crime family. Operated out of the Blue Collar Inn in Garfield, N.J., the racket proffered loans to small businessmen, manual laborers and others at exorbitant interest rates. The loans were backed by large and menacing mob "enforcers." Bruschi's operations extended to at least seven North and Central Jersey counties and included illegal sports betting. They were connected to a central "wire room" in New York, which coordinated betting and loan activities in the two states. Evidence was unearthed indicating that the New York Genovese and Lucchese crime families cooperated in dividing up the North Jersey market in these rackets.[14]

North Jersey's labor unions have offered New York's mob families other profit centers. Members of organizations such as Local 69 of the Hotel Employees and Restaurant Employees International Union have been victimized. Headquartered in Secaucus, Local 69 is alleged to have been infiltrated by members and associates of the Genovese crime family. Among the alleged Genovese rackets are embezzlement of union funds, extortion of employers who use union labor, and extortion of union members' rights. Leaders of Local 69 were accused of complicity in illegal activities and of promoting an atmosphere of intimidation among members.[15] The problem reached such proportions that in 2002 a federal court appointed a special monitor to oversee the union's activities.

As if Gotham's gangland enterprises weren't enough, Philadelphia's Bruno/Scarfo mob families have also maintained operations in New Jersey for many years.[16] Much smaller in scale, though, they appear to have confined their North Jersey operations largely to Newark and Atlantic City.[17] However, internal gang conflict and the imprisonment of mob boss Nicodemo D. Scarfo have undercut their activities since the 1990s. Philadelphia's mob received another blow in 2002 when Scarfo's son was convicted of organizing and heading a gambling operation from a North Jersey office; the conviction came about in part through decrypted computer records obtained by the FBI.[18]

Although organized crime continues to infect life in North Jersey, many of the senior mobsters are either in prison or are succumbing to age or illness. For example, Louis "Streaky" Gatto Sr., an octogenarian and a former North Jersey captain in the Genovese crime family, died in 2002 while serving a sixty-five-year prison term for gambling rackets.[19] At the top, Joseph "Joe Bananas" Bonnano, once head of the Bonnano family, and John "Dapper Don" Gotti, an imprisoned ex-head of the Gambino family, have also expired.[20] By 2003 Gotti's successor and the heads of the other four New York crime families were all in prison.[21] Still, several mid- and high-level members of the Lucchese, Gambino, and Genovese families completed prison sentences in 2002 and

2003 and their members are thought to remain active.[22] Meanwhile, gangsters with ties to Korea, Cuba, and the former Soviet Union have infiltrated.[23]

A BIG-TIME WANNABE: THE DECAVALCANTE FAMILY

Clearly, external organized crime families have dominated the rackets in North Jersey. But the escapades of the DeCavalcante family, New Jersey's only indigenous, traditional organized crime unit, may illustrate why serious underworld activity is best left to out-of-state gangsters. Organized in the 1960s, the DeCavalcante family made its living from extortion, bribery, and bogus stock transactions, among other rackets. A favorite enterprise was bribing or extorting local officials to obtain building permits for construction company clients. After an FBI investigation, Don Simone Rizzo "Sam the Plumber" DeCavalcante served prison time on gambling charges, later retired to Florida, and died in 1969 at the age of eighty-four.[24] One source characterized him as a "sort of gofer" for the Mafia commission in New York.[25] DeCavalcante was succeeded by several bosses, all of whom were toppled from power or imprisoned.[26]

Although members of the five New York crime families vastly outnumbered the DeCavalcante mob, they generally avoided conflict with their homegrown counterparts, hoping not to draw official attention to their operations. But whatever annoyances the North Jersey gang may have posed to their more powerful rivals, disintegration from within became a more serious problem. With time, the DeCavalcante mob was termed "a wretched parody of itself" by one veteran reporter and "certainly not the A Team" by a federal investigator.[27]

The DeCavalcantes were plagued by two habits: their violence and their blunders. For example, a few members murdered their boss when they suspected that he was gay, fearing that other gangs would not respect them. Murders became so routine that it was necessary for the DeCavalcante gang to hire a man for the sole purpose of disposing of the victims' bodies in another state. One former head of the gang admitted to having given orders to kill more than a dozen people. Despite their popular image, the New York mobs generally employed murder more sparingly than the DeCavalcantes, because they sought to avoid generating heat from the press and law enforcement authorities.[28]

At least as troubling to the DeCavalcante family was the litany of gaffs and goofs that undermined their stature. One story describes a former underboss found dead in his car with a jar of fish in his lap. Whatever the fish symbolized, its significance escaped everyone in the gang. In another incident, two gang members inadvertently shot each other as they sat in a car waiting to kill another man. In a third incident, FBI officials secretly planted cell phones with gang members who used them for months, never realizing that their conversations were being recorded. Finally, the police saw one member dispose of a murder weapon; the member was later identified by the license plates on his car. It turned out that he had stolen the plates from a vehicle belonging to the wife of another mob member. Her husband was soon held for questioning and the hapless bumbler was later dispatched by the gang.[29]

The DeCavalcante family's continual antics and perpetual bloodshed have relegated them to a second-banana status among Greater New York's Mafia families.[30] One measure of this status is the fact that no DeCavalcante gang member is believed ever to have sat on the syndicate or commission that rules the five New York families and oversees Mafia operations in New Jersey.[31]

NORTH JERSEY AND YOU, TONY, PERFECT TOGETHER

Perhaps to the relief of many North Jerseyans, mob activity in Greater New York has been associated for generations in the public mind primarily with New York City. As the headquarters city of the Mafia, New York has been the setting for countless Hollywood films, television shows, books, and magazine articles about organized crime. Perhaps this is why the HBO series *The Sopranos* has raised emotions running from amusement to chagrin among New Jersey viewers. A weekly series about the mobster, Tony Soprano and his family, friends, and criminal associates, *The Sopranos* is set in the affluent suburbs and grimy strip malls of North Jersey. *The Sopranos* confirmed in popular culture what had been a fact, at least in the northeastern United States, for a generation or more—that mob activity was no longer confined to cities and had, indeed, penetrated well beyond them. But the show could not be set in just any metropolitan area. The producers at HBO apparently decided that the North Jersey suburbs of Manhattan provided a more persuasive locale for a gangster saga than, for example, those of Connecticut, Long Island, Cleveland, or Los Angeles. *The Sopranos*, first telecast in 1998, seems to confirm that public realities and popular perceptions regarding North Jersey's long history of organized crime have, at last, converged.

POLITICAL CORRUPTION

If organized crime has raised concerns about image in New Jersey, it is not the only vice to do so. Over the past two centuries, from the state's heyday as a canal, railroad, and manufacturing center to its present-day global economy, a cavalcade of corrupt politicians has inflicted damage on civic life.[32] These circumstances would be less remarkable were it not for the fact that the

Garden State has been served by many honorable public officials, including governors such as Woodrow Wilson, Brendan Byrne, Tom Kean, and Christie Whitman and members of Congress such as Bill Bradley, Peter Rodino, and Millicent Fenwick. Similarly, citizens have been blessed with no shortage of worthy and dedicated leaders in the statehouse, court houses, and county and municipal offices.[33] And yet, New Jersey has suffered a long legacy of political misbehavior undermining public confidence in government. Nowhere is this reputation more ingrained than in North Jersey, where the U.S. Attorney's Office has waged an aggressive war on organized crime and political corruption for decades.

GARDEN-VARIETY GRAFT IN THE GARDEN STATE

Essex County, with the largest city (Newark) and the second-largest county population in the state, illustrates North Jersey's political corruption dilemmas. In recent years several county officials have been indicted or convicted for political misdeeds (Table 1, pp. 130–35). In 2003 James W. Treffinger, a Republican and the Essex County Executive, was convicted of mail fraud and obstructing justice. Treffinger admitted that he had solicited an illegal $15,000 campaign contribution in exchange for awarding a county no-bid paving contract. He also confessed to placing two people in county jobs who then worked full time on his reelection campaign.[34] Ironically, a decade earlier Treffinger had succeeded County Executive Thomas D'Alessio, a Democrat, who had been convicted of money-laundering and accepting a bribe from an out-of-state trash hauler who wanted a New Jersey license. As if these improprieties weren't enough, once released from prison, D'Alessio formed a nonprofit charitable fund with leftover political campaign funds, paying himself an annual salary of more than $65,000. He placed family members and friends on the board of the organization and drove a Mercedes Benz leased by the fund.[35] D'Allesio's post-prison actions were perfectly legal under New Jersey law at the time.

Having two successive Executives convicted of corruption would be enough for most counties, but graft in Essex County runs deeper. In 2002 former Newark Mayor Kenneth Gibson was convicted of federal income tax evasion for failing to report earnings that would have resulted in an additional $78,000 in tax payments. Gibson admitted that his engineering firm billed the Irvington, New Jersey school board for more than $1 million in services never performed. Newark's first black mayor was placed on probation for his crimes. Two former members of Irvington's school board confessed to accepting payoffs from Gibson for their support in landing the school construction contract.[36] Like Treffinger, Gibson had managed to sustain a pattern perpetuated by an unknown number of mayoral predecessors. One of the more prominent of them was Newark Mayor Hugh J. Addonizio, who was convicted in 1970 of corruption in office and served time in prison.[37]

Yet, the skullduggery in Irvington, a severely troubled older community bordering Newark, ran deeper than Gibson's crimes. In 2003 Irvington Mayor Sara Bost was found guilty of prevailing upon a town employee to lie to federal investigators about a city paving contract. Based on wiretaps and other evidence, she was indicted for accepting a $1,500 kickback from the contractor in 1999 and $7,000 in bribes from the developers of an apartment complex in the town.[38] She pleaded guilty to attempted witness tampering and was sentenced to one year's imprisonment.[39]

Another North Jersey urban center, Passaic County, has also been the target of federal officials. Most prominently, Martin Barnes, once mayor of Paterson, admitted in 2002 to accepting more than $200,000 in bribes. Six city contractors were involved, including a paving company with more than $16 million in Paterson contracts. Principals in the paving firm confessed to paying for fourteen free trips for Barnes and his guests to such places as Aruba, Rio de Janeiro, and England. During the travel, federal officials charged, Barnes was accompanied by his wife, a girlfriend, or hired female companions. Other gifts included clothes, cash, and home improvements.[40] But the graft didn't stop at the mayor's door. In 2002 Conway Mangullo, Paterson's director of public works, was found guilty of receiving $7,500 in extortion money in return for issuing a new city contract to a paper goods vendor.[41]

Mayor Barnes, like Treffinger, was not the first politician in his county to succumb to temptation. As recently as 2000, Passaic County's administrative head, Nicola DiDonna, pleaded guilty to conspiracy charges in a scheme involving the award of county contracts to a consulting company. The consultant, in turn, paid kickbacks to politically connected individuals selected by Republican Party head Peter A. Murphy. Murphy, who admitted having a financial interest in the consulting firm, was convicted for arranging $3 million in county contracts to a firm that had paid bribes totaling more than $70,000 to four Murphy political allies.[42] These and other party loyalists have operated in a climate of widespread corruption. In fact, election improprieties in Passaic County became so blatant that beginning in 1999 federal monitors were posted at voting booths to thwart intimidation of Hispanic voters and poll workers.[43]

Doubtless, some observers have suspected that law enforcement actions such as these are politically or racially motivated. However, North Jersey's experience in recent years shows that the politically corrupt are partial to no particular ideology, skin color, sex, or nationality. Indeed, the subregion's political felons are collectively a bipartisan, bigender, biracial, and multiethnic crowd—proving that some temptations are just too attractive to allow little things to get in the way.

If North Jersey's governmental misdeeds were infrequent, perhaps their influence on popular perceptions inside and outside the state would be less severe. But the evidence is substantial that the state, and especially the subregion, suffer in the public eye. In 2003 a poll showed that 77 percent of New Jerseyans believed that the state had "a lot" or "some" political corruption, while 15 percent said there was "only a little" or "none." (A year earlier another survey found that 84 percent believed that some or a lot of corruption existed in New Jersey.) Respondents in the 2003 poll opined that on average about one-half of politicians are corrupt.[44] A 2002 survey found that nearly two-thirds of New Jerseyans believed that elected officials go into politics for personal gain.[45] In 1981 another survey provided a benchmark suggesting that for the most part opinions have changed little over the past two decades.[46]

Perhaps public perceptions such as these help to explain the response of a retiring Newark city councilman when he was asked to name his greatest accomplishment after twenty-eight years of service in that capacity. It was not that he had supported important reforms in government, put affordable housing in neighborhoods, or improved public parks, for example. The councilman replied, "I've never been the subject of an investigation. No one has accused me of stealing any money or being a crook."[47] So inured to corruption have many North Jerseyans become that a double negative may indeed be considered a positive.

The corrosive effects of political corruption have marred the reputation of government in the state, and especially in North Jersey. New Jersey's former attorney general, John Farmer, has acknowledged the problem. The state, he said, harbors "an ingrained culture of corruption," noting that even after many attempts to clean it up a "margin of rascality persists."[48] The state's largest newspaper, the *Star-Ledger*, has editorialized against "the worst stereotypes of New Jersey—that we shrug and wink at corruption, that New Jersey's culture makes it inevitable, that we are somehow unable to clean our own house."[49] And, the *New York Times* has referred to the state's reputation "as a place where graft remains as much a part of life as diners, toll-booths, Springsteen and 'The Sopranos.' "[50] In another story, the same *Times* reporter referred to the state's "reputation for slimy politics."[51]

Similar characterizations come from outside the region. For example, the *Los Angeles Times* referred to "corruption that has long been a fixture in the Garden State." Noting that "corruption is pervasive," the newspaper quoted New Jersey's U.S. Attorney that the problem is "almost an epidemic."[52] As long ago as 1974 *The Almanac of American Politics*, which examined politics in all fifty states, described New Jersey as "the nation's most corrupt state."[53] In 2003 the *Economist* magazine, referring to another state with a similar reputation, called New Jersey the "Louisiana of the north."[54] And during the 2004 presidential election campaign, candidate Ralph Nader declared that in New Jersey, elections, politicians, the state government and many municipal governments are "for sale."[55]

Regardless of these perceptions, there is little, if any, objective evidence indicating that the Garden State ranks particularly high nationally in incidents of political misbehavior.[56] Nevertheless, if North Jersey has spawned the most extensive record of political corruption and organized crime in the state, perhaps Hudson County, home to Hoboken, Jersey City, and ten other communities, is its most natural habitat. A closer examination sheds more light on these matters, and, at the same time, shows how the postindustrial era is bringing momentous changes to North Jersey's economic, social and political landscapes.

Figure 20. Jersey City's Goldman Sachs tower (far left) symbolizes the "Manhattanization" of North Jersey's waterfront. Once filled with longshoremen and factory workers, the city is now home to bond traders, financial planners, lawyers, and accountants.

HUDSON COUNTY HIJINKS

If the city of Newark were looking for a model for renewing itself, it might look no further than neighboring Hudson County (Map 3, p. 43). Two of North Jersey's most successful cities, Hoboken and Jersey City, are well on the way to reinventing themselves. In doing so, they are leaving behind their blue-collar, manufacturing past and embracing a white-collar, postmodern future.[57] Both cities lie on the so-called Gold Coast, a strip along the Hudson River with spectacular views of Manhattan's spiky skyline. Many of their residents commute easily by ferry, bus, or rail to jobs on Wall Street or in Midtown. Others work elsewhere in North Jersey or in Jersey City's burgeoning finance, insurance, and real estate sectors. By 2000 Jersey City was the second-largest employment center in New Jersey, having added about six thousand jobs over the 1990s.[58] With a 2000 population of more than 38,000, Hobo-

Figure 21. Abandoned pilings offer testimony to North Jersey's once-vibrant working water-front. Living in the shadow of Gotham, many of today's residents work in midtown Manhattan or the Wall Street financial district.

ken is primarily residential in character, with rows of brownstone townhouses and apartment buildings, a commuter rail station, and many upscale bars, restaurants and retail shops. Jersey City is both an employment center and a collection of residential neighborhoods. Once lined with clanging railroads, smoky factories, and busy wharves, its waterfront is now walled by a row of gleaming office towers built mostly since the late 1980s. Jersey City's population, about 240,000 in 2000, includes those living in converted factories and warehouses, brick townhouses, condominiums and apartment towers in several gentrified neighborhoods. Lacing the two cities together is a new surface rail transit line running more or less parallel to the Hudson River waterfront.

Both cities have undergone drastic transitions since the late 1970s and 1980s. Because gentrification expanded first in Hoboken, however, its population is about four-fifths white, while Jersey City's populace is only one-third white. The proportions of

African Americans and Hispanics living in Hoboken are far smaller than in Jersey City. Levels of educational achievement are much higher there, while the shares of foreign-born and poor people are considerably lower.[59]

Formerly teeming with smokestacks, trucks, warehouses, and corner bars, the two communities still show evidence of their blue-collar past. But yesterday's industrial loft is today's high-end condominium complex. And the corner bar is now a hip-hop night club or a brew pub. Briefcases and backpacks have replaced lunch pails and thermos bottles and the scent of pierogies, goulash, and corned beef and cabbage has been supplanted by the fragrance of pad thai, fajitas, and garlic bagels. Where scenes for *On the Waterfront* were filmed in the 1950s, inline skaters, cyclists, and sunbathers today relax in a scenic waterfront park. And where Colgate toothpaste, Dixon pencils, and Clorox bleach were once produced amid rolling conveyors, steaming vats, and spinning blades, today real estate transactions, stock purchases, and financial plans are crafted in the air-conditioned suites of Goldman Sachs, Merrill Lynch, and Paine Webber.

It is becoming increasingly difficult to think of Hoboken and Jersey City as the quintessentially North Jersey factory towns they once were, so closely are their destinies now linked to Manhattan's office-worker economy.[60] Beginning in the 1970s and 1980s Hoboken—and to a lesser extent Jersey City—became spillover locales for young workers, many of whom couldn't afford the more desirable neighborhoods of Manhattan and Brooklyn. By the mid-1990s, young people were being priced out of Hoboken and the back offices of financial services firms were being priced out of Lower Manhattan's crowded canyons. Both began to overflow into Jersey City. Realtors now refer to the two cities collectively as "the sixth borough of New York" and to Jersey City's office enclave as "Wall Street West." Stories of their revivals, so remarkable to those who remember the grimy Hoboken and Jersey City of yore,

Figure 22. An artifact from Jersey City's industrial past stands in stark contrast to the revitalizing neighborhood surrounding it.

Figure 23. The new Jersey City, composed of office towers, residential complexes, eateries, and retail shops, is a vast departure from the gritty age of smokestacks, assembly lines, corner bars, and union halls.

Figure 24. The Empire State Building, Manhattan's most identifiable landmark, rises dream-like over the city's skyline. Cyclists, inline skaters, runners, and walkers find inspiration along Hoboken's new waterfront.

have been told in similar form in American cities such as Baltimore, Cleveland, Lowell, and Providence.

Gentrification began in the neighborhoods near the waterfront in both cities and gradually spread westward. Organizations were formed to protect historic buildings, press for better urban design, and open public access to the waterfront. In Jersey City, older neighborhoods such as Journal Square and Greenville have been joined by elite developments named Port Liberte, Portofino, and Marbella. Yet culturally diverse enclaves persist, such as the Martin Luther King Bergen/Lafayette neighborhood and Little India, a strip of restaurants and shops wafting scents of curry and ginger. In some sections of the two cities, however, brownfields betray a very different past. Abandoned warehouses, rusting rail yards, and pockmarked streets lie awaiting redevelopment, not for families who have lived there for generations but for newcomers with mobile phones, laptop computers, and MP3 players.

Figure 25. Hoboken, once home to the crooner Frank Sinatra, clings to its ethnic past even as formerly dowdy storefronts offer lattes, smoothies, sushi, and designer shoes.

JERSEY CITY'S DON OF POLITICAL CORRUPTION

Although revitalization has improved many smaller communities in North and Central Jersey, nowhere has the process been more dramatic than along the Gold Coast. Yet, the glitter cannot com-

Figure 26. Despite revitalization in this neighborhood, homes such as this one reflect the attachment of some Hoboken working-class families to familiar places, neighbors, and institutions.

pletely mask old habits and traditions that once cast all of Hudson County in a very different light. No one will ever know the full story of the county's long history of political corruption.[61] But most people agree that it reached its most illustrious heights during the reign of Frank "The Boss" Hague, the mayor of Jersey City

Figure 27. Gentrification has transformed legions of Hoboken townhouses such as these into trendy homes for young working singles and couples.

from 1917 to 1947. Hague's infamy among American big-city mayors earned him the rank of second only to Chicago's William "Big Bill" Thompson on a list of the "worst mayors" in America.[62] A machine boss of Olympian authority, Hague has been called "an urban tyrant" who used "strong arm tactics" like a "warlord over a fiefdom."[63] He also served as the head of Hudson County's Democratic machine for many years, a job giving him power over Democratic politicians in the county.

Under Hague's rule, city and county employee rolls were padded with excess workers who served the party. Three-percent salary kickbacks to the machine were expected from each of these minions. No-show jobs were plentiful, embarrassing public records were concealed from public scrutiny, city contracts were let only in return for kickbacks to the machine, and bidding processes were rigged to favor contractors supportive of "The Boss." Hague dealt ruthlessly with those who got in his way, including public employees, many of whom were fired or demoted. To protect his party loyalists from legal action, Hague manipulated appointments to judgeships and public attorney positions, securing jobs for those who took a benign view of machine practices.[64] One account, from a woman who grew up in Jersey City over the last one-third of the twentieth century, describes Hague's vindictiveness: "Hague knew at all times what was happening on his streets. Phones were tapped, mail was opened, and spies lurked at Bickford's, a popular Journal Square cafeteria. And, always, the traitors were punished. His critics would find their right to vote revoked or their tax assessments raised, and if they were especially feisty, they'd be beaten and then arrested for 'sarcastic criticism of superiors.'"[65]

"The Boss" was able to get away with these deeds for thirty years, in part because city services were generally efficient and his machine was usually responsive to constituent needs. But these benefits came at the price of an enormously bloated budget.[66] And like voters in most machine cities at the time, Jersey City's population was substantially made up of the "poor, the ill-educated, and the unskilled," who were "socially amenable to machine politics."[67] In the time-honored tradition of city bosses, then, Hague persisted mainly because the voters allowed him to do so. He died in the mid-1950s, his salary never exceeding $9,000 annually. But his estate amounted to $5 million in assets, plus luxury properties in New Jersey, New York City, and Palm Beach, Florida. Remarkably, he was never imprisoned. In the decades following Hague's regime, mayors such as John V. Kenny and Thomas J. Whelan were convicted for their own misdoings, although neither ever earned the accolades or opprobrium directed to their illustrious predecessor.[68]

POSTMODERN POLITICAL PERFIDY

As the manufacturing economy declined, Hoboken and Jersey City lost their smokestacks and chemical smells and began to attract notice from young home seekers and office developers. Soon, corporate leaders in financial services and middle-class college graduates brought different political expectations. Although dishonesty in office persisted, it was no longer possible to maintain the bloated machine payrolls and frequent payoffs common in an earlier day. And thanks to more aggressive law enforcement, Hudson County's miscreants were being prosecuted. A bellwether of the changing mood was the trial of Jersey City mayor Gerald McCann in the early 1990s. He was convicted of fraud, income tax evasion, and perjury.[69] He was succeeded by the conservative Brett Schundler, the first Republican mayor of Jersey City since World War I, who served from 1992 to 2001. A young reformer, the Harvard-educated Schundler presided over a record period of growth and development in the city helped by an aggressive national economy and a generous tax abatement policy for developers. Yet, even Schundler's example of clean government in Jersey City could not erase a culture of corruption in Hudson County. Next door, Mayor Anthony Russo of Hoboken was practicing business as usual. He succeeded in getting himself convicted in 2004 for accepting more than $300,000 in bribes from firms seeking contracts with the city.[70] Between 1997 and 2003 at least twelve public officials or police officers in Hudson County were convicted of accepting bribes, passing bribes, embezzling, tax improprieties, and/or misappropriation of campaign funds (Table 1).[71]

At the top was the conviction of the Hudson County Executive and two members of the County Board of Freeholders beginning in 2002. County Executive Robert Janiszewski confessed to extorting in excess of $100,000 in return for his support in awarding county contracts.[72] One of his associates, who had been a Jersey City police officer for thirty-two years, Freeholder William Braker, pleaded guilty to receiving nearly $4,000 in cash and political contributions from a psychiatrist seeking his vote to approve a county health-services contract. Heard on a police wiretap recording, Braker, when asked by the man what he wanted in return for his vote, replied, "Cash and Viagra."[73] Another freeholder, Nidia

TABLE 1. Political Corruption in North Jersey, 1990–2005

Name of convicted	Title/Office at Time of Crime	Jurisdiction Represented	County	Convicted of (Crimes)	Year Crimes Committed	Year of Conviction	Description of Misdeeds
Janiszewski, Robert	County executive	Hudson	Hudson	Extortion and tax evasion	1996–2001	2002	Received over $100,000 from contractors providing services to the county
Colon, Nidia Davila	County freeholder	Hudson	Hudson	Fraud and aiding extortion	1999	2003	Assisted an extortion attempt and mail fraud; passed at least $10,000 in bribes from contractors to the county executive; lied to FBI agents
Braker, William	County freeholder and ex-police officer	Hudson	Hudson	Accepting kickbacks from contractor	2000	2004	Extorted contractor for nearly $5,000
Russo, Anthony	Mayor, 1993–2001	Hoboken	Hudson	Extortion and bribery	1995–2000	2004	Accepted at least $317,000 in exchange for city contracts for accounting services

Name	Position	Municipality	County	Charge	Dates	Year	Details
Auriemma, Joseph	Township administrator	North Bergen	Hudson	Bribery	1993–2000	2002	Auriemma, Hernandez, and Perez accepted free home renovations from contractors and cash bribes
Hernandez Joseph	Purchasing agent	North Bergen	Hudson	Bribery	1990–2000	2002	
Perez, Peter	Township commissioner	North Bergen	Hudson	Bribery	1995–97	2002	
Zappulla, Vincent	Town aide	North Bergen	Hudson	Mail fraud	1996–97	2002	Insurance scam
Mango, Albert	Former chair of the North Bergen planning board	North Bergen	Hudson	Bribery	2000	2001	Solicited and accepted bribes
Abreu, Rene	Aide to mayor	West New York	Hudson	Extortion	Late 1990s	Indicted 2002	A witness claims he conveyed bribe money from illegal gambling operator to a highly placed local official
6 unnamed policemen	Police chief and officers	West New York	Hudson	Bribery	Mid-1990s	Late 1990s	Bribery to protect illegal prostitution and gambling businesses
Vartan, Leo	Mayor, lawyer, and former Hudson County prosecutor	Kearny	Hudson	Embezzlement and tax evasion	Late 1990s	2002	Embezzled campaign reelection funds in 1997 ($20,000 to $70,000 for personal use) and failed to report money on his income tax return

TABLE 1 (Continued)

Name of convicted	Title/Office at Time of Crime	Jurisdiction Represented	County	Convicted of (Crimes)	Year Crimes Committed	Year of Conviction	Description of Misdeeds
Lavilla, Peter	Mayor	Guttenberg	Hudson	Tax evasion	1996–98	2003	Misappropriated campaign contributions for use in trading personal stocks
D'Agosta, Frank	Police detective	Jersey City	Hudson	Extortion	2002–3	2003	Collected payoffs from operator of illegal lottery in return for protecting the racket
Anderson, Jean	Deputy registrar, Vital Statistics Office	Hudson	Hudson	Conspiracy	2000	2004	Provided false birth certificates to Razendra Bohadur, who paid Anderson, then sold them to Nikhil Goswamy; Goswamy convicted of illegally transferring false documents in 2004
Impreveduto, Anthony	Assemblyman for 17 years; member of ethics committee	N.J. State Legislature	Hudson (elected from)	Misuse and misrepresenting of political campaign funds	1999–2004	2004	Used campaign funds to pay for at least 2 trips abroad, furniture, a hearing aid, eye-glasses, income tax liabilities; at least $50,000 misused

Name	Position	Municipality	County	Charge			Description
Treffinger, James	County executive	Essex County	Essex	Mail fraud and obstructing justice	2000	2003	Solicited $15,000 illegal campaign contribution in exchange for awarding a county no-bid paving contract; placed 2 people in county jobs who worked on his reelection campaign
D'Alessio, Thomas	County executive; chair of county Democratic organization	Essex County	Essex	Money-laundering and accepting bribe	Early 1990s	1994	Accepted a $59,000 bribe from an out-of-state trash hauler for N.J. license
Gibson, Kenneth	Mayor, 1971–86	Newark	Essex	Tax fraud	1993	2002	Failed to report income that would have resulted in an additional $78,000 tax payment; his engineering firm billed Irvington, N.J. school board for over $1 million in services never performed
Fuller, David	Business administrator; president of school board	Irvington	Essex	Accepted kickbacks from contractors	Late 1990s	2001	Received bribes from Kenneth Gibson to maintain contract

TABLE 1 (Continued)

Name of convicted	Title/Office at Time of Crime	Jurisdiction Represented	County	Convicted of (Crimes)	Year Crimes Committed	Year of Conviction	Description of Misdeeds
Silas, Donald	School board member	Irvington	Essex	Witness tampering	Late 1990s	2001	Urged others to lie about receiving bribes
Bost, Sara	Mayor, 1994–2002; former Essex County freeholder	Irvington	Essex	Witness tampering; plea deal led to reduced charges	1999	2003	Accepted $1,500 kickback from contractor in 1999 and $7,000 in bribes from developers of an apartment complex; prevailed on city employee to lie to federal investigators about a city paving contract
Barnes, Martin	Mayor	Paterson	Passaic	Mail fraud, tax fraud	2000	2002	Accepted over $200,000 in bribes from 6 contractors including a paving company with $16 million in contracts. Accepted 14 free trips, gifts (clothes, cash, and home improvements) and hired female companionship

Name	Position	Place	County	Charge	Years	Year	Description
DiDonna, Nicola	County administrator	Passaic County	Passaic	Conspiracy to commit mail fraud	1993–97	2000	Conspiracy in a scheme involving county award of contracts to a consulting company paying kickbacks to a county political party official
Murphy, Peter A.	Republican Party leader	N.A.	Passaic	Mail fraud	1994–98	2001	Arranged $3 million contracts for nursing and drug-testing services to a firm that paid bribes totaling over $70,000 to 4 Murphy political allies; after serving one year, his sentence was vacated
Mangullo, Conway	Public works director	Paterson	Passaic	Extortion	1997–2001	2002	Received $7,500 extortion money in return for issuing a new city contract to a paper goods vendor
Talley, Charles	Housing Authority commissioner	Plainfield	Union	Extortion	1995–96	2000	Demanded $10,000+ from developer in exchange for his support to build a health-care facility
Davis, Richard H.	Business administrator	Wykoff Board of Education	Bergen	Embezzlement, conspiracy to conceal financial transactions	1993	2001	Paid town contractor more than $1.7 million for services never rendered and divided the money with contractor

SOURCE: Newspaper files and press releases, U.S. Attorney's Office, Newark, N.J.

Davila Colon, was convicted of mail fraud and passing at least $10,000 in bribes to Janiszewski, which she had received from the same psychiatrist. At the time, she was in a personal relationship with the briber, although she did not know that he was wearing a wiretap device.[74] Several others were also indicted or convicted, including a developer, an accountant, and a county aide to Janiszewski.[75] Once again, corruption was an equal opportunity employer; Janiszewski is a white Polish American, Braker an African American and Davila Colon a Hispanic.

HUDSON COUNTY HOODLUMS

Probably no one would claim that official dishonesty is extinct in Hudson County. But it may be an endangered species. So, too—apparently—are the activities of the mob. In fact, some people believe that there is a relationship between the two. But, as the old-style political machines of North Jersey have largely faded from the scene, so also have the opportunities for mobsters to seek protection for their rackets through payoffs and other schemes. Without the cooperation of crooked mayors, council members, police, and other officials, gambling, loansharking, and prostitution are difficult to sustain. But, like trace elements in a geological sample, organized crime is detected every now and then. Perhaps the most tenacious of the New York-based rackets remaining in Hudson County is centered next door to Jersey City in Bayonne. Local 1588 of the International Longshoremen's Association is headquartered there.

Under the control of the Genovese crime family, Local 1588 has been associated with multiple crimes over the past three decades. Union leaders were charged with requiring members who wanted promotions, overtime pay, or job training to pay kickbacks to the mob. Those who held no-show jobs in the union were required to forfeit a portion of their salary. Shipping company executives were threatened with longshoreman labor unrest if they did not pay extortion money. Genovese employees such as "Benny Eggs" Mangano and "Johnny Sausage" Barbato allegedly collected a "tariff" of $25 for each container off-loaded from a ship.[76] Even union pension funds and prescription drug benefits were manipulated to the benefit of the Genovese organization, according to accusations. In recent years at least four heads of Local 1588 have been found guilty of crimes such as embezzling union funds.[77] A federal judge has placed the union under the temporary control of a former head of the New York City police department.[78]

Not all of Hudson County's gangsters are waterfront entrepreneurs. A former Jersey City resident named Elvis Irizzary, an organized crime enforcer, was convicted in 2001 for multiple murders. Among his victims were two men in North Bergen in 1993; his ex-girlfriend's son in Bayonne in 1997; a man in Brooklyn in 1993; and a fifth man in Jersey City in 1994. He stabbed one victim more than forty times and stalked another on the street, shooting him in the back of the head. In addition, Irizzary received convictions for torching two houses in Jersey City and an automobile in Newark, for robbery in Brooklyn, and for loansharking and cocaine distribution.[79]

Yet, when mob violence arises, it is usually less dramatic than this. In the case of Joseph "Joe Curley" Taglianetti, attempts to collect protection money from the owner of a Bayonne automotive tinting shop and garage proved his undoing. The mobster was sentenced in 2003 to forty-six months of imprisonment for heading a conspiracy to commit extortion and threaten physical harm. Taglianetti's enforcer, Frank "Big Frank" Pastore, was sentenced to thirty-nine months of incarceration.[80]

GOODFELLAS, GRAFTERS, AND THE IMAGE OF CORRUPTION

The twin dilemmas of political corruption and organized crime seem to have taproots running all the way to the core of North

Jersey's identity. Both curses have persisted for generations and few believe that they will disappear any time soon. To their credit, the mass media, reform organizations, and federal and state authorities labor tirelessly to diminish the influence of "goodfellas" and grafters. While many people express dismay when the activities of mobsters and hacks are exposed, another dimension of public reaction roughly approximates prurient interest in sex. There is, after all, something both forbidden and titillating about the high and mighty being toppled from their governmental perches—and likewise for the low and mighty being uprooted from their underworld lairs. While North Jerseyans would likely agree that crooked politicians and gangsters do not speak well for the subregion, many betray a good-natured resignation to their presence. Generations of Jerseyans have endured jokes about the state's highways, pollution, slums, litter, and the like. What, they seem to think, would put North Jersey on the map, were it not for devious politicians and thugs? Although North Jersey has scenic mountains, none are as grand as those outside Denver. It has lakes, but they are far less impressive than those gracing Minneapolis, Cleveland, or Toronto. Like Chicagoans, North Jerseyans enjoy a majestic skyline, but it belongs to Manhattan, not Newark, Paterson, Elizabeth, or Jersey City. Despite the subregion's affluence, high level of educational attainment, and many illustrious current and former inhabitants, it still contends with a long heritage of crooked pols and polished crooks. Attitudes among North Jerseyans about these matters range from perverse amusement to weary resignation. For some, there is nothing more dearly loved than a good, tongue-clucking scandal. For others, perhaps, there is this: Damn other states, for it is more interesting to be noted for oily officials and menacing mobsters than for corn production, cheese tonnage, or longhorn cattle.

Image, Identity, Dominion

This book portrays North Jersey as a subregion of Greater New York whose social, cultural, political, and economic contours have been molded both from within and from without. Within the state there has been an enduring struggle between *pluribus* and *unum,* between the mandates of collective responsibility and the fulfillment of individual purpose. The complexities of race, class, ethnicity, nationality, and religion have helped to shape this struggle—and increasingly, so have the limitations of localism, land, and natural resources. Overlaying these primarily internal struggles is a compelling series of trans-Hudson tensions, rooted largely in politics and economics and propelled variously by cooperation, competition, or an amalgam of the two. The peculiar conditions of local news and professional sports in North Jersey offer insights into how perceptions of place and culture are overshadowed by the sheer dominance of Manhattan-based enterprises. Furthermore, political corruption and organized crime illustrate how civic pride and trust in government can be undermined from within and from without.

Yet, this portrait of the Manhattan-North Jersey axis of Greater New York is not a static one. As New Jersey's population and business environments have grown, the balance of economic and political power between Manhattan and its North Jersey suburbs has shifted somewhat.[1] These forces, in turn, have strengthened the hand of the Garden State's governmental and business leaders in resolving cross-border issues. Consequently, today's leaders parry and thrust with their Big Apple governmental and corporate counterparts on firmer footing than their predecessors did in the 1960s or 1970s. Not only has New Jersey's white-collar economy grown, the expansion of the global economy has significantly altered its makeup. Corporate capital in pharmaceuticals and health, entertainment, high technology, financial services, and real estate is adapting to new national and international orders. One result is that the once sharply demarcated lines of authority that gave New York City such influence over many aspects of North Jersey life have abraded to some degree. As two economists have characterized it, New Jerseyans "have built a kind of 'fire wall' between the suburbs and the city," leaving them "less vulnerable (and) more diversified."[2]

Yet, the long reach of Manhattan still exerts a powerful influence over many aspects of life in North Jersey. Where Manhattan forces once exerted power over North Jersey under royal and colonial governments, today mass media, professional sports, and organized crime empires have forged market-based forms of power through the cooperation—be it enthusiastic, indifferent, or reluctant—of Garden State consumers. Moreover, reducing the disparities in economic and political power between Manhattan and North Jersey has come at a price. To accommodate their new population and industries, North Jersey communities traded land and natural resources, primarily for economic advantage. However, this advantage was maldistributed, with the newer suburbanizing counties (Morris, Sussex, Warren, Hunterdon, and Somerset) of Outer North Jersey becoming the primary economic counterweight to the New York City economy. Today, Outer North Jersey forms an arc on the western and southern perimeters of Inner North Jersey.[3] Meanwhile, the five more urbanized counties

of Inner North Jersey suffered rising racial and socioeconomic isolation, economic decline, and physical decay. While Inner North
Jersey continues to encompass vast differences in economic advantage and cultural identity, Outer North Jersey displays a more
affluent, less diverse social profile. Perhaps what most sets Inner
and Outer North Jersey apart is the spatial proximity of difference:
Despite Inner North Jersey's several exclusive and relatively ho-
mogenous communities, most of its residents are never far re-
moved from those of a different race, ethnicity, or religion. But in
Outer North Jersey, sprawl has put greater distance—and perhaps
greater apathy (if not hostility)—between people of dissimilar circumstances.

Edge cities, post-suburban sprawl, highways, larger vehicles
and homes, and yes, even larger people, have gobbled countless
acres of North Jersey's remaining open space. As they have done
so, they have diminished the natural realm in ways that challenge
the subregion's long-term sustainability. State and local governments continue to pursue jobs, income, tax revenues, and shiny
new buildings. And politicians and planners, who waltzed to the
tune of comprehensive planning in the 1970s, growth management in the 1980s, and smart growth in the 1990s, skitter about
searching for new lyrics as each verse succumbs to the discordant
strains of politics and economics. In all cases North Jerseyans test
what may be the limits of human propinquity. Small wonder then,
that a 1999 poll revealed that only 14 percent of state residents
agreed that New Jersey's then-thirteen-year-old program to man-
age growth had been successful; nearly three times as many (39
percent) thought it was not successful, while the remainder (47
percent) found it of mixed success.[4]

Further confounding the picture, a pattern of granulated local
governments has undermined the capacity of citizens and politicians to deal effectively with the challenges of development. Over
the past thirty years, state government has raised its profile in

issues of growth, but it remains to be seen whether the political will is up to the challenge. Growth in many North Jersey communities has become much like alcohol dependency: just as one drink leads to the next and the next, so also does one more subdivision or shopping center lead to another and another. While growth has enabled North Jersey partially to offset the long reach of Manhattan, the full effects of associated land and natural resources costs are yet to be confronted.

BEING NORTH JERSEY

Though North Jersey's growth has loosened Manhattan's grip on the subregion's political and economic stature over the past thirty years, Gotham remains an international center of business, fashion, the mass media, entertainment, and culture. In this respect, it has transcended the status of a mere city and become a global commodity, whose products, services, and images are in demand worldwide. So powerful is Gotham's reach that its impacts on surrounding suburbs can be compared to few other central cities in the United States. The results of a 2003 survey, however, indicate that not all who live in North Jersey view these influences as undesirable. The study found that a higher share of North Jerseyans (75 percent) rated the state an "excellent" or "good" place to live than did Central (69 percent) or South (68 percent) Jerseyans. Conversely, higher shares of Central (31 percent) and South (32 percent) Jerseyans rated the state "only fair" or "poor" compared to North Jerseyans (24 percent).[5]

Similarly, when asked how they compared their own state to most other states as a place to live, a larger share of North Jerseyans (34 percent) responded that New Jersey was "better" than did their counterparts in Central (30 percent) or South (25 percent) Jersey. Furthermore, more North Jerseyans (53 percent) indicated that they take "a lot" of pride in being a resident of the state than did those living in Central (45 percent) or South Jersey (51 percent). When asked whether on the whole they thought New Jersey's image among outsiders was positive or negative, 50 percent of Northerners termed it positive and 46 percent negative. Central and South Jerseyans were somewhat more likely to rate the outside view of the state negatively.[6] Similar results were obtained in another poll in 2001.[7] Although these disparities are not large, they suggest that living near Manhattan is considered a plus by many North Jerseyans.[8] So, even though Manhattan influences have done much to discourage a stronger sense of place and identity in North Jersey, they bring compensations that many residents appear to value.

One reason is that, in effect, numerous North Jerseyans are "dual citizens" of the Garden State and Gotham. Many thousands work in New York, periodically visit the city, and/or harbor memories of once having lived there.[9] Of course, not all residents feel this way and some are as indifferent, if not hostile, to Gotham as like-minded souls in Kansas or Mississippi.[10] Yet, no matter how much or how little North Jerseyans visit Manhattan, their perspectives on self and community are indisputably influenced to some degree by its economic, political, and cultural exports.

Manhattan has achieved the status of a center stage in the world community. As a global capital, it draws the eyes and ears of the planet through films and commercials set in New York, television broadcasts from its studios, and financial transactions on Wall Street. The arts and artifacts of the world appear in its galleries and museums, and performers worldwide find their way to its stages. Moreover, each year millions of tourists travel from many corners of the world to walk Manhattan's streets. Put simply, as a global commodity, Manhattan is always in the camera's eye.

But behind the camera's eye is another realm. Those who live outside Manhattan in Greater New York know it well. It is in some respects a subworld struggling to behave much like the rest of metropolitan America, with Little League baseball games, PTA meetings, and backyard barbeques. But it is also a region in which much of human experience is filtered through a world lens forever fixed on Manhattan's people, places, and events. While being near Manhattan brings opportunities to suburbanites, it also detracts from the formation of a strong sense of place and cultural identity in North Jersey. As a result, to be a North Jerseyan in the shadow of Gotham is to live in a divided dominion in which, perhaps, too few aspects of life can be termed distinctively "Jersey."

Still, to say that North Jersey has struggled in the shadow of Gotham is not to suggest that it has done so in isolation. In particular, Inner North Jersey shares many facets of its identity with the nearby boroughs of Brooklyn, Queens, and the Bronx.[11] They all contain dozens of neighborhoods of closely packed homes, corner bars, pop-and-mom stores, neighborhood restaurants, working and abandoned factories, and people of richly diverse cultural backgrounds. And all suffer second-banana status on a stage where Manhattan forever plays the starring role. Generations of observers—from vaudeville to films to novelists to the Comedy Central cable channel—have exploited North Jersey and the boroughs for laughs. In some cases, quintessential New Yorkers, themselves, take aim. In the movie *Sleeper*, for example, Woody Allen pokes fun: "I'm what you would call a teleological, existential atheist. I believe that there's an intelligence to the universe, with the exception of certain parts of New Jersey."[12] Likewise, Calvin Trillin has his say: "He pretended to concentrate on his newspaper although he was, in fact, still thinking of the state of New Jersey, which he envisioned as a series of vast shopping-mall parking lots, where any fool could find a spot."[13] In other cases, the levity comes from more distant sources, such as a *Miami Herald* columnist: "The United States is developing an odor bomb. 'Why?' you are saying. 'Don't we already have New Jersey?'"[14]

Conversely, the image of Manhattan from North Jersey more often takes on a respectful, sometimes reverential, quality. For example, another New Yorker reflected on his youth in North Jersey and the siren call of the Manhattan skyline. "When I reached a hilltop vista which looked far out over the Hackensack Meadows, I loved to sit and stare at that fantasy rising miles and miles away through the mists. From that distance it seemed to me as dreamlike as the Emerald City of Oz."[15]

All too often, it seems, humor arises as much from the fact that the boroughs and North Jersey are *not* Manhattan as from the fact that they *are* the places they are.[16] Despite similarities, though, Brooklyn, Queens, and the Bronx have an indelible advantage over North Jersey: though they may be "stepchildren" of Manhattan, they are still "family," if by nothing more than the "marriage" of New York City's municipal consolidation in 1898. North Jersey, in contrast, is related to Manhattan neither by blood nor wedlock. So North Jerseyans sometimes find their subregion portrayed as something akin to the neighborhood's bastard child. As such, North Jersey is just a bit more likely than the boroughs to score a perfect ten on the laugh meter of life.

CELEBRATING NORTH JERSEY

Even though North Jersey has groped with many challenges over its existence, none of these tell the whole story for they don't explain why New Jersey continues to grow, even as neighboring states continue to lose population. What is it that lures people to the Garden State year after year? Clearly, North Jersey's proximity to Manhattan and its many career opportunities, shopping venues, and cultural assets are important attractions. But does this mean that North Jersey's appeal is limited strictly to its associations with the Big Apple? Hardly.

Most visitors would probably agree that few, if any, of the subregion's inland assets—its lakes, mountains, or woodlands—are the equal of those in neighboring New York State or Pennsylvania. But they are more accessible to many New Yorkers, as well as New Jerseyans, who continue to visit them year after year. And the Jersey shore draws tens of thousands of tourists from upstate New York and Pennsylvania, neither of which has similar lengths of sandy beaches. So, the sheer convenience of North Jersey's natural open spaces contributes to the attractiveness of life in the subregion.

Then there is North Jersey's community life. Long ago, much of the spirit of New England culture seeped southward, borne by settlers in North Jersey's villages and hamlets. Today, granulated government and post-suburbanism aside, one can find dozens of small communities with attractive downtowns, friendly shopkeepers, interesting topography, pleasant homes, and congenial neighbors. Jazz, folk, rock, and classical music concerts and festivals abound. Reenactments of battles of the Revolutionary War, aerobatics demonstrations, and hot-air balloon meets are annual events. Arts and crafts shows are held regularly. And lovers of classic cars, chopper bikes, antiques, modernist furniture, old movies, long-playing albums, and 1950s diners find a welcoming home. Put simply, the rich, textured, variegated, and quirky stuff of life is everywhere apparent in North Jersey.

Another way to gauge the appeal of North Jersey is to consider who has called the state home over the years. The list of accomplished Americans who have resided in the Garden State is a long one. Setting aside George Washington, Alexander Hamilton, Aaron Burr, and several signers of the Declaration of Independence, a selective accounting of its more illustrious citizens includes the inventors Thomas Edison and Samuel F. B. Morse; the political cartoonist Thomas Nast; the Nobel Prize-winning physicist Albert Einstein; Presidents Grover Cleveland and Woodrow Wilson (a former New Jersey Governor); authors Stephen Crane and Edmund Wilson; the poets Walt Whitman, William Carlos Williams, and Joyce Kilmer; the musician William Count Basie; the abolitionist Harriet Tubman; the actor Paul Robeson, and the comedians Bud Abbott, Lou Costello, and Jerry Lewis. Among prominent New Jerseyans of the late twentieth century are the jazz musician Dizzy Gillespie; the singers Sarah Vaughan, Whitney Houston, Dionne Warwick, Connie Francis, Jon Bon Jovi, and Paul Simon; the poets Amiri Baraka (LeRoi Jones) and Alan Ginsberg; the authors Norman Mailer and Philip Roth; the actresses Meryl Streep, Olympia Dukakis, and Queen Latifah; the actors Joe Piscopo, Joe Pesci, Bruce Willis, Kevin Spacey, John Travolta, Danny DeVito, Tom Cruise, and Jack Nicolson; the astronaut Edwin "Buzz" Aldrin; the rapper Ice-T; the athlete Shaquille O'Neal; and the home-decorating mogul Martha Stewart.[17]

Yet, of all its "alumni" perhaps none is so celebrated as Frank Sinatra and Bruce Springsteen. Both are native sons of the Garden State and both are lionized by millions of fans worldwide. While Sinatra was raised in North Jersey's Hoboken, Springsteen grew up in Freehold, just south of the subregion (as defined here). Both singers hailed from working-class backgrounds and both achieved astonishing success, albeit largely among white audiences. Known respectively as "the Chairman of the Board," and "the Boss," Sinatra and Springsteen have had signature effects on American popular culture. Between them, their music has captured generations, from the bobby-soxers of the 1940s to current rock fans.

Although both men have been popular with large numbers of Garden Staters, it was Springsteen who most successfully wove his Jersey origins into his art. Many of his songs bespeak the realities of life in the state. In his song "State Trooper," from the 1982 *Nebraska* album, he memorializes the New Jersey Turnpike: "New Jersey Turnpike, ridin' on a wet night 'neath the refin'ry's glow / Out where the great black rivers flow."[18] In "Rosalita," from the *The Wild, the Innocent, and the E-Street Shuffle* (1973), "the Boss" bespeaks a different aspect of New Jersey's car culture: "My tires were slashed and I almost crashed but the Lord had mercy / My machine she's a dud out stuck in the mud somewhere in the swamps of Jersey."[19] And in "Atlantic City," also from *Nebraska*, Springsteen sings of a night on the town in New Jersey: "Put your makeup on, fix your hair up pretty, / Meet me tonight in Atlantic City."[20]

Many of Springsteen's fans live in North Jersey and his tunes resonate with them. He conveys the pleasure, the perils, the laughter, and the longing of Jersey life with humility and warmth. Perhaps by drawing so heavily from his Jersey roots, Springsteen has discovered some near-universal aspects of life in an increasingly homogenized America. But underlying the scenes he creates with his musical paintbrush is a respect for people everywhere whose lives were supposed to deliver just a little bit more. It is the image, if not the reality, of this perpetual underdog status that seems to resonate with Springsteen's North Jersey fans.

There are signs that the subregion's multimillion dollar homes, high-ranking incomes, exclusive neighborhoods, illustrious citizens, and rich history have somewhat softened the dark shadows cast by Gotham. And yet comparisons are impossible to escape. So many North Jerseyans work at jobs tied in some way to the New York City economy. So many more are influenced by what they absorb from the city's many media empires. To seek relief in movies or sports is only to be reminded once again that the settings and the teams are far more often identified with Gotham than with the Garden State. Precisely because of these influences, perhaps, Springsteen's lyrics have cast light on life in North Jersey and found something indigenous and genuine to celebrate.

NOTES

Prologue

1. John Brooks, "The Meadows," in *A New Jersey Reader* (New Brunswick, N.J.: Rutgers University Press, 1961), 3–25.

2. Robert Sullivan, *The Meadowlands: Wilderness Adventures on the Edge of a City* (New York: Doubleday, Anchor Books, 1999), 143–45.

3. Ibid., 153–63.

4. Ibid., 168–71.

5. Brooks, 4, 8.

6. Ibid., 7.

7. Sullivan, 93–106.

Chapter 1

1. The U.S. Census Bureau estimated that New Jersey's population in 2004 reached nearly 8,700,000, adding nearly 285,000 people since 2000. See Robert Gebeloff, "The State We Love to Leave," *Star-Ledger,* April 15, 2005, 1.

2. Some geographical characterizations refer only to North and South Jersey, dividing the state in its middle. See, for example, Kevin Coyne, "Across the Great Divide," *New Jersey Monthly* 30 (2005): 1: 48–51. Others identify a small band of counties in mid-state as Central Jersey. Although I deal mostly with North Jersey in this book, my references to Central Jersey generally encompass Mercer, Middlesex, and Monmouth counties. The university towns of Princeton and New Brunswick and the retail and advanced services employment corridor located astride Route 1 lie in Central Jersey. South Jersey would thus include Burlington, Ocean, Camden, Gloucester, Atlantic, Salem, Cumberland, and Cape May coun-

ties. Although I do not do so here, some observers might prefer that the four Atlantic coastal counties be identified as the Jersey Shore, a separate subregion.

3. Exact measures of North Jerseyans employed in Manhattan are difficult to find. One source indicates that in 2000 nearly 308,000 New Jerseyans worked in New York City. See Rae D. Rosen, senior economist, Federal Reserve Bank of New York, presentation to the Value of Cities International Conference, London, October 16, 2003, retrieved January 21, 2005 at http://www.london.gov.uk/mayor/ economic_unit/value_cities_presentations / NewYork_RaeRosen.rtf. Another source indicates that in 2001 nearly 323,000 New Jersey workers were employed in New York State. See New York Adjusted Gross Income and Tax Liability, Office of Tax Policy Analysis, New York State Department of Taxation and Finance, Annual Statistical Report, September 2004, retrieved January 21, 2005 at http:// www.tax.state.ny.us/pdf/stats/Stat_Pit/COR/analysis_of_2001_ny_state_ personal_income_tax_returns_by_place_residence. ptf. Data from the 2000 Census indicate that more than 252,000 New Jersey workers commuted daily to Manhattan. See Steve Chambers and Robert Gebeloff, "A Suburban Crossroads Becomes Boom Town," *Star-Ledger,* December 31, 2003, 1, 6.

4. Jean Gottmann, *Megalopolis: The Urbanized Northeastern Seaboard of the United States* (New York: The Twentieth Century Fund, 1961).

5. See, for example, Susan S. Fainstein, *The City Builders: Property, Politics, and Planning in London and New York* (Lawrence: University Press of Kansas, 1994), and Janet L. Abu-Lughod, *New York, Chicago, Los Angeles: America's Global Cities* (Minneapolis and Saint Paul: University of Minnesota Press, 1999).

6. Charles A. Stansfield, Jr., *New Jersey: A Geography* (Boulder, Colo.: Westview Press, 1983), 21, and Thomas Fleming, *New Jersey: A Bicentennial History* (New York: W. W. Norton and Co., Inc., 1977). According to Fleming (14–16), it took a trial in English courts to finally rid Perth Amboy of the duties imposed from New York.

7. Stansfield, 22.

8. Stanley N. Worten, Wilbur E. Apgar, Daniel Jacobson, and Abraham Resnick, *New Jersey: Past and Present* (New York: Hayden Book Co., Inc., 1964), 52–58.

9. Fleming, 85–86. As a small state, New Jersey wanted an equal number of congressional representatives from each of the states, regardless of size or popula-

tion. Larger states such as New York called for proportional representation to reflect their larger number of voters. The Great Compromise resulted in an equal number of members per state in the Senate and proportional representation in the House of Representatives.

10. Worten, et al., 59–63; Fleming, 82–85.

11. Fleming, 98.

12. John E. Pomfret, *Colonial New Jersey: A History* (New York: Charles Scribner's Sons, 1973), 200.

13. Fleming, 93, 112

14. Jameson W. Doig, *Empire on the Hudson: Entrepreneurial Vision and Political Power at the Port of New York Authority* (New York: Columbia University Press, 2001), 69. In all, portions of twelve New York and New Jersey counties were included in the Authority's jurisdiction.

15. Doig, 71–119.

16. Jerome H. Cranmer, *New Jersey in the Automobile Age: A History of Transportation* (Princeton, N.J.: D. Van Nostrand Co., Inc., 1964), 38–39.

17. Doig, 113.

18. Cranmer, 69, and the Port of New York Authority, *Nineteenth Annual Report* (1939): 31–32, 38.

19. Cranmer, 70–72, and the Port of New York Authority, *Nineteenth Annual Report,* 34–36, 50–51.

20. Cranmer, 73–78, and the Port of New York Authority, *Nineteenth Annual Report,* 39, 50.

21. Angus Kress Gillespie, *Twin Towers: The Life of New York City's World Trade Center* (New Brunswick, N.J.: Rutgers University Press, 1999), 25–30.

22. Cranmer, 73–78.

23. The Port of New York Authority, *Thirty-first Annual Report* (1951): 35–36.

24. Ibid., 86–92.

25. Kenneth T. Jackson, *Crabgrass Frontier: The Suburbanization of the United States* (New York and Oxford: Oxford University Press, 1985), 268.

26. Doig, 382–92; Gillespie, 35–40.

27. The Port of New York Authority, *Annual Report* (1962): 32–39.

28. Doig, 385–88.

29. Ibid., 385–90.

30. Port Authority of New York and New Jersey, *Meeting the Global Challenge: Comprehensive Annual Financial Report* (1989): 18.

31. Port Authority of New York and New Jersey, *Annual Report* (1984): 7–8.

32. Mark Mueller and Mary Jo Patterson, "The Final, Terrible Toll from the Trade Center: 2,749," *Star-Ledger,* January 24, 2004, 3. See also "In Bereavement, Pioneers Along a Lonely Trail Search for Peace," *New York Times,* September 8, 2002, 28.

33. Michael N. Danielson and Jameson W. Doig, *New York: The Politics of Urban Regional Development* (Berkeley and Los Angeles: University of California Press, 1982), 151–53. For a closer analysis of the MRC's failures, see Jon Teaford, *Post-Suburbia: Government and Politics in the Edge Cities* (Baltimore: John Hopkins University Press, 1997), 118–19.

34. Excerpts from the Supreme Court's Decision on Ellis Island, *New York Times,* May 27, 1998, B7 (Proquest Historical Newspapers).

35. "New York's Title to Ellis Island," *New York Times,* January 13, 1998, A18 (Proquest Historical Newspapers).

36. Ibid. For an account of the Ellis Island controversy see Gerald Benjamin and Richard P. Nathan, *Regionalism and Realism: A Study of Governments in the New York Metropolitan Area* (Washington, D.C.: Brookings Institution Press, 2001), 34–35.

37. "Ellis Island," *Microsoft Encarta Online Encyclopedia 2004,* http://encarta.msn.com. See also www.saveellisisland.org. Since the Court's decision, a New Jersey panel has prepared a plan recommending that facilities to house international conferences and centers be built. Among the purposes recommended are the study of immigrant contributions, ethnic learning, public health, conservation and preservation, and the Hudson River Valley history.

38. Charles V. Bagli, "Budget Crisis Ends Program That Lured Jobs to New Jersey," *New York Times,* January 31, 2003, B1, B7.

39. Charles V. Bagli, "Goldman Asks for Grants Downtown," *New York Times,* December 12, 2003, B1–B8.

40. Ibid.

41. David M. Herszenhorn, "Tax Plan for Non-Residents Aims at Where the Money

ls," *New York Times,* November 16, 2002, B4; Ron Marsico, "Jerseyans May Be
Hit by Commuter Tax," *Star-Ledger,* September 5, 2002, 1; Robert Schwaneberg
and Jeff Whelan, "Jersey Weighs Options to Thwart Revival of N.Y. Commuter
Tax," *Star-Ledger,* September 6, 2002, 37.

42. Jeff Whelan, "McGreevy Halts Talks about Transfer Station for N.Y. Garbage,"
Star-Ledger, February 18, 2004, 11.

43. A slightly different characterization was offered by Bob Yaro, head of the Regional Plan Association, an organization concerned with planning issues in the
New York area. He termed the relationship between New York and New Jersey
"like plate tectonics," suggesting the seismic and unpredictable nature of bi-
state politics. Author's notes, Meeting of the Regional Plan Association, New
Jersey Committee, May 16, 2002, Elizabeth, N.J.

44. Fleming, 204.

45. An example of such political momentum is the pressure on the New York State
and New Jersey congressional delegations to cooperate on behalf of issues of
mutual concern. Since the 1970s both states have lost members of the House of
Representatives through congressional redistricting to sunbelt states with growing populations. As their total number of votes in the 435-member House has
declined, members from New York State and New Jersey have had greater incentives to find common cause.

Chapter 2

1. Michael N. Danielson and Jameson W. Doig, *New York: The Politics of Urban
Regional Development* (Berkeley and Los Angeles: University of California Press,
1982), 262–64.

2. U.S. Census Bureau, Table 30, "Large Metropolitan Areas—Population: 1980–
2000," *Statistical Abstract of the United States* (2002): 32.

3. Peter O. Wacker, *Land and People: A Cultural Geography of New Jersey: Origins
and Settlement Patterns* (New Brunswick, N.J.: Rutgers University Press, 1975),
74–81. See also Richard P. McCormick, *New Jersey: From Colony to State,* rev.
ed. (Newark: New Jersey Historical Society, 1981), 1–9

4. McCormick, 1.

5. Ibid., 37.

6. Wacker, 50.

7. Ibid., 201–3.

8. Thomas Fleming, *New Jersey: A Bicentennial History* (New York: W. W. Norton and Company, Inc., 1977), 115.

9. McCormick, 23–27.

10. Ibid., 93.

11. Ibid., 80. The author observed that by 1786 New Jersey was home to 36,000 Presbyterians (24 percent), 24,000 Quakers (16 percent), 24,000 Dutch Reformed (16 percent), 15,000 Calvinists (10 percent), 12,000 Lutherans (8 percent), 12,000 Baptists (8 percent), 10,000 Episcopalians (6.7 percent), and much smaller numbers of Mennonites and Roman Catholics. More than 14,600 people (almost 10 percent) were thought to be of no religious affiliation.

12. McCormick, 81.

13. Ibid.

14. Fleming, 129.

15. Charles A. Stansfield, Jr., *New Jersey: A Geography* (Boulder, Colo.: Westview Press, 1983), 59. For a study of New Jersey immigrant groups, see David Steven Cohen, ed., *America, the Dream of My Life* (New Brunswick, N.J.: Rutgers University Press, 1990).

16. Brian Donohue, "Immigrant Wave Continues to Wash onto N.J. Shores," *Star-Ledger,* July 15, 2003, 13. The data list both those who arrived in New Jersey as legal immigrants and those living in the state who became legal immigrants through the Immigration and Naturalization Service.

17. Brian Donohue and Robert Gebeloff, "A Clearer Portrait of Hispanics," *Star-Ledger,* May 6, 2003, 25.

18. Brian Donohue and Robert Gebeloff, "Census Traces a Path of Skill and Success to the Philippines," *Star-Ledger,* April 29, 2003, 1.

19. Robert Gebeloff, "Immigrants Keep N.J. Population Growing," *Star-Ledger,* April 17, 2003, 19.

20. Robert Gebeloff, "Census Spells Out More Diverse State," *Star-Ledger,* September 18, 2003, 29.

21. Ted Sherman, "Jersey's Dwindling European Heritage," *Star-Ledger,* May 26,

2002, 1. The Census Bureau data are based on self-identity by respondents in the 1990 and 2000 censuses; respondents were allowed to indicate several countries of ancestry, although only the first two are recorded. Thus, the totals yield a higher number than the actual population of the state.

22. Brian Donohue, "Jersey's Immigrant Ranks Surge," *Star-Ledger,* September 20, 2002, 1.

23. These figures are from the 2000 decennial census. More recent estimates from the Census Bureau suggest that the population of Georgia has surpassed New Jersey's and that the population of North Carolina will do so soon. If true, the Garden State would now be the tenth or eleventh most populous nationally. See Robert Gebeloff, "It May Seem Crowded, but Jersey Growth Lags," *Star-Ledger,* December 22, 2004, 19.

24. Jonathan Casiano, "Still Flocking to the Land of Opportunity," *Star-Ledger,* November 27, 2002, 2. In 2001 New Jersey received nearly sixty thousand immigrants, surpassing runners-up Illinois, Massachusetts, Virginia, Washington State, and Maryland. With immigrants making up 18.5 percent of the state's population, New Jersey has proportionally the third-largest concentration of non-natives in the nation after California and New York.

25. U.S. Census Bureau, "State and County QuickFacts," New Jersey Data Center, http://quickfacts.census.gov/qfd/states/34000.html.

26. One source has computed an Index of Dissimilarity, a widely respected measure of racial segregation, for U.S. cities and metropolitan areas. The index measuring segregation between blacks and whites in 2000 was 77.8 in Newark and 80.4 in the Newark metropolitan area. A value above 60 is considered very high. See "Metropolitan Racial and Ethnic Change—Census 2000," Lewis Mumford Center State University of New York at Albany, retrieved on January 21, 2005 at http://mumford1.dyndns.org/cen2000/wholePop/WPSegdata/564omsa.htm.

27. Tables (2001) from "Newark, N.J. PMSA—Data for the Metropolitan Statistical Area," and "Newark City—School Segregation Data for the School District Area," Lewis Mumford Center of the State University of New York at Albany. Retrieved on December 12, 2005 at http://www.albany.edu/mumford/census.

28. U.S. Census Bureau (2000), "Montclair Township, Essex County, New Jersey,"

American FactFinder, retrieved December 12, 2005 at http://factfinder.census.gov.

29. U.S. Census Bureau, Census 2000, Summary File 1, Matrix P1. Retrieved December 12, 2005 at http://factfinder.census.gov.

30. Lise Funderberg, "Integration Anxiety," *New York Times Magazine,* November 17, 1999, 85.

31. Ibid., 87.

32. In nearby South Orange and Maplewood, adjacent communities that share a single high school, efforts to forge a racially balanced community and school system have encountered new challenges. (See the Prologue.) There, conflict has arisen over the practice of assigning students to classes based on measured ability. Often, blacks are assigned to classes with lower performance expectations and whites to those that are more rigorous. Black students and parents complain that racial separation occurs, while white parents argue that mixed classes bring lower standards of achievement and boredom for their children. These tensions have raised fears that more whites will send their children to private schools. While Maplewood's 2000 population was about two-thirds white and one-third black, its 2005 high school enrollment was 58 percent black and 35 percent white. In both Montclair and Maplewood-South Orange, anxieties exist that the delicately maintained goals for social justice will falter. See Jeffrey Gettleman, "The Segregated Classrooms of a Proudly Diverse School," *New York Times,* April 3, 2005, 31.

Chapter 3

1. Kenneth Jackson, *Crabgrass Frontier: The Suburbanization of the United States* (New York: Oxford University Press, 1985). See also Lizabeth Cohen, *A Consumer's Republic: The Politics of Mass Consumption in Postwar America* (New York: Alfred A. Knopf, Borzoi Books, 2003).

2. James Howard Kunstler, *Home from Nowhere* (New York: Simon and Schuster, 1996), 257.

3. Dennis E. Gale, "Eight State-Sponsored Growth Management Programs: A Comparative Analysis," *Journal of the American Planning Association* 58, no. 4

(1992): 425–39. New Jersey's growth management law, enacted in 1986, is commonly referred to as the State Planning Act.

4. For a general history of the three Mt. Laurel cases and their aftermaths, see David Kirp, John P. Dwyer, and Larry A. Rosenthal, *Our Town: Race, Housing, and the Soul of Suburbia* (New Brunswick, N.J.: Rutgers University Press, 1995).

5. Ibid.

6. Department of Environmental Protection, State of New Jersey, Final Report of the New Jersey Comprehensive Risk Project, Trenton, N.J., March 16, 2004. Retrieved January 14, 2005 at http://www.state.nj.us/dep/dsr/njcrp/.

7. Robert Gebeloff, "Jersey's Out-of-the-Way Places Are Now the Way Home," *Star-Ledger,* July 10, 2003, 1.

8. Laura Mansnerus, "New Jersey Is Running Out of Open Land It Can Build On," *New York Times,* May 24, 2003, B1.

9. Kristen Alloway, "Report Fears for Vanishing Highlands," *Star-Ledger,* April 5, 2002, 27.

10. "A New Vision for the Highlands," *New Jersey Future*, no. 5 (February 2004): 1, retrieved December 21, 2005 at http://www.njfuture.org.

11. David Kocieniewski, "In Trenton, a Sweeping Act to Protect the Highlands," *New York Times,* June 11, 2004, B6.

12. Steve Chambers, "As Open Space Shrinks, Public Sounds Stumped," *Sunday Star-Ledger,* Sept. 29, 2002, 1. See also "Sprawl Is Top Threat, New Jersey Voters Say 2–1," Quinnipiac University poll, retrieved May 29, 2004 at http://www.quinnipiac.edu/x4274.xml.

13. Alexander Lane, "Census: Big Erosion of State Farms," *Star-Ledger,* June 4, 2004, 23.

14. Steve Chambers, "Million-Acre Promise Stalls," *Sunday Star-Ledger,* August 3, 2003, 1.

15. Ibid.

16. Andre Malok, "New Jersey's Black Bear," *Star-Ledger,* September 22, 2002, 26–27.

17. Brian T. Murray, "To Bears, There's No Place Like Jersey," *Star-Ledger,* September 22, 2002, 1.

18. Alexander Lane, "From One Barrier to Next, Bob the Bear Ambles South," *Star-Ledger,* June 18, 2002, 1.

19. Brian T. Murray, "State Hosts Conference on Bears," *Star-Ledger,* March 3, 2003, 31.

20. Kristen Alloway, "Hanover Begins Killing Off Geese at Sewage Plant," *Star-Ledger,* June 25, 2002, 34.

21. Adding to New Jersey's environmental dilemmas, the state has a high number of hazardous waste sites. In 2001 it ranked first in the nation with 116 such sites. See U.S. Census Bureau, Table 357, "Hazardous Waste Sites on the National Priority List by State: 2001," *Statistical Abstract of the United States* (2002): 22.

22. Anthony S. Twyman, "DEP's Computer Map Shows Pollution Endangering Water Wells," *Star-Ledger,* September 26, 2002, 27.

23. Lawrence Ragonese, "Cut in Watershed Aid Hurts Northwestern Towns," *Star-Ledger,* July 9, 2002, 29.

24. John M. Payne, "Fairly Sharing Affordable Housing Obligations: The Mount Laurel Matrix," *Western New England Law Review* 22 (2001): 365–80. See also Kirp, et al.

25. Kathy Barrett Carter, "Challenge Is Rebuffed on Affordable Housing," *Star-Ledger,* April 29, 2004, 20.

26. David Kocieniewski, "Critics Say Housing Proposal Would Worsen a Shortage," *New York Times,* August 27, 2003, B5.

27. Joel Garreau notes that New Jersey does not have "even one major city. Whatever their virtues, Newark and Elizabeth are rarely described as big time." He adds that the "central reality of New Jersey [is] Edge Cities." See Joel Garreau, *Edge City: Life on the New Frontier* (New York: Doubleday, Anchor Books, 1991), 25.

28. John E. Bebout and Ronald J. Grele, *Where Cities Meet: The Urbanization of New Jersey,* New Jersey Historical Series, vol. 22 (Princeton, N.J.: D. Van Nostrand Co., Inc.), 5–7, 93–95. The authors refer metaphorically to this pattern of crustal urbanization as the "City of New Jersey" (95–99).

29. U.S. Census Bureau, Table 33, "Incorporated Places with 100,000 or More Inhabitants in 2000—Population, 1970 to 2000, and Land Area, 2000," *Statistical Abstract of the United States* (2002): 36–38.

30. These data from the 2000 Census were obtained from the website of the Joseph

C. Cornwall Center for Metropolitan Studies at the Newark campus of Rutgers: The State University of New Jersey, Newark, N.J. and were retrieved March 4, 2003 at http://www.cornwall.rutgers.edu.

31. U.S. Census Bureau, Table 30, "Large Metropolitan Areas—Population: 1980– 2000," *Statistical Abstract of the United States* (2002): 32. My use of the term metropolitan areas includes both Metropolitan Statistical Areas and Primary Metropolitan Statistical Areas as defined by the Bureau of the Census.

32. Bebout and Grele, 93–95.

33. Peter Dreier, Todd Swanstrom, and John Mollenkopf, *Place Matters: Metropolitics for the 21st Century,* 2d ed. (Lawrence: University Press of Kansas, 2004).

34. Jon Teaford, *Post-Suburbia: Government and Politics in the Edge Cities* (Baltimore: John Hopkins University Press, 1997).

35. Steve Chambers, and Robert Gebeloff, "Jersey's Scattershot Commute," *Star-Ledger,* March 6, 2003, 1. This article describes a study showing that five of the twenty counties nationally with the "most chaotic" commuting patterns were in the northern half of New Jersey.

36. Joel Garreau, *Edge City: Life on the New Frontier* (New York: Doubleday, Anchor Books, 1991).

37. Bebout and Grele, 14, 27–28, 61–65.

38. Ibid., 62.

39. For a recent summation of New Jersey's extensive experience with municipal incorporation, exclusionary zoning, and class exclusivity, see Jeffrey M. Stonecash, with Mary P. McGuire, *The Emergence of State Government: Parties and New Jersey Politics, 1950–2000* (Madison and Teaneck, N.J.: Fairleigh Dickinson University Press, 2003), 17, 38.

40. Gregory R. Weiher, *The Fractured Metropolis: Political Fragmentation and Metropolitan Segregation* (Albany: State University of New York Press, 1991), 3. See also Michael N. Danielson, *The Politics of Exclusion* (New York: Columbia University Press, 1976); Jon Teaford, *City and Suburb: The Political Fragmentation of Metropolitan America, 1850–1970* (Baltimore: John Hopkins University Press); and Gary J. Miller, *Cities by Contract: The Politics of Incorporation* (Cambridge, Mass.: MIT Press, 1981).

41. Michael N. Danielson and Jameson W. Doig, *New York: The Politics of Urban*

Regional Development (Berkeley and Los Angeles: University of California Press, 1982), 100–105.

42. Ibid., 78–94. See also Weiher, 13–15.

43. Alan J. Karcher, *New Jersey's Multiple Municipal Madness* (New Brunswick, N.J.: Rutgers University Press, 1999), 70, and Stonecash with McGuire, 38. See also Robert Strauss, "Municipal Madness or Creative Localism," *New York Times*, New Jersey Section, January 4, 2004, 6.

44. U.S. Census Bureau, Table 335, "Land and Water Area of States and Other Entities," *Statistical Abstract of the United States* (2002): 210, and U.S. Census Bureau, Table 406, "Number of Local Governments by Type—States," *Statistical Abstract of the United States* (2002): 261. Both tables can be found at http://quickfacts.census.gov/gfd/states/34/34039.html.

45. Robert C. Wood and Raymond Vernon, *Anatomy of a Metropolis: The Changing Distribution of People and Jobs within the New York Metropolitan Region* (Cambridge, Mass.: Harvard University Press, 1959). See also Raymond Vernon, *Metropolis 1985* (Cambridge, Mass.: Harvard University Press, 1960); Robert C. Wood, with Vladimir V. Almendinger, *1400 Governments: The Political Economy of the New York Metropolitan Region* (Cambridge, Mass..: Harvard University Press, 1961), 24–26, 51–57, 104–13; Myron Orfield, *American Metropolitics: The New Suburban Reality* (Washington, D.C.: The Brookings Institution, 2002), 130–33.

46. Weiher, 14–19, 59–60, 168–69. See also Danielson, 43–46, 125, 156, 164–65, 285–86.

47. See Transactional Records Clearinghouse, Syracuse University at http://trac.syr.edu/tracirs/findings/aboutTP/states/NewJersey/counties. See also Al Frank, "Morris Ranks with Wealthiest U.S. Counties," *Star-Ledger*, April 27, 2004, 43. In another source Morristown and the edge cities are identified as part of New Jersey's "wealth belt" of affluent suburban and exurban communities. See James W. Hughes, Joseph J. Seneca, and Connie O. Hughes, "Anticipating Census 2000: New Jersey's Emerging Demographic Profile," *Rutgers Regional Report* (Edward J. Bloustein School of Planning and Public Policy, Rutgers University) issue paper no. 18 (July 2000): 12.

48. Data from the Lewis Mumford Center, University of Albany, "Metropolitan Racial and Ethnic Change—Census 2000," for Morris School District, File on Ethnic and

Racial Composition, retrieved June 20, 2004 at http://mumford1.dyndns.org/
cen2000/SchoolPop/SdistSegdata/3410810sd.htm.

49. Matthew J. Dowling, "'Bad Boys' Tied to Bias Attacks on Hispanics," *Star-Ledger*,
September 29, 2004, 15; Bill Swayze and Paula Saha, "2 Students Cut in School
Cafeteria Brawl," *Star-Ledger*, October 9, 2003, 25. In Paterson thirteen African
American teens were convicted on various charges in the beating death of a
homeless Hispanic man. See Rudy Larini, "Teen Guilty in Fatal 'Wilding Spree,'"
Star-Ledger, October 21, 2004, 21. See also Damien Cave, "A Question of Hate,
or Full Pockets?" *New York Times*, October 24, 2004, 29.

50. Bill Swayze, "Workers' Gathering Location Revisited," *Star-Ledger*, June 15,
2003, 29.

51. Eugene Mulero, "Police Issue Warnings to Morris Day Laborers," *Daily Record*,
April 12, 2005, A1; Bill Swayze, "Crackdown on Contractors Draws Protests,"
Star-Ledger, April 12, 2005, 23.

52. Tom, Feeney, "A Town's Human Dilemma," *Star-Ledger*, November 4, 2003, 1;
Bob Braun, "In Freehold: Our Hometown, Not Theirs," *Star-Ledger*, December 17,
2003, 17; "Some Oppose New Job Hall for Migrants in Freehold," *New York
Times*, January 3, 2004, B2.

53. Bruce Lambert, "Advocates for Immigrants Say Suffolk Officials Foster Bias,"
New York Times, August 2, 2003, B5.

54. Garreau, 26–29, 39–40.

55. One long-time student of urban design cites the Morristown–Parsippany–Troy
Hills area as "almost accidental," but nevertheless "a new city." See Jonathan
Barnett, *The Fractured Metropolis* (New York: HarperCollins Publishers, Icon Edi-
tions, 1995), 3, 17.

56. Garreau, 40, refers to the Morristown area as an "incipient" edge city.

57. Steve Chambers and Robert Gebeloff, "A Suburban Crossroads Becomes Boom
Town," *Star-Ledger*, December 31, 2003, 1.

Chapter 4

1. For a study on the portrayal of urban crime in two large American cities, see
Daniel Yanich, "Location, Location, Location: Urban and Suburban Crime on
Local TV News," *Journal of Urban Affairs* 23, nos. 3–4 (July 2001): 221–42.

2. Eagleton Poll Archive, Poll 123, questions qgv14 and qgv16, September 1999,

retrieved January 23, 2005 at http://www.scc.rutgers.edu/eagleton/
serverFreq.cfm?quest_Quest_ID_453058 820.

3. There is some evidence that at least in North Jersey, many viewers think that
their television coverage tends to overemphasize more sensational events. A
survey of New Jersey's registered voters in 1999 revealed that less than one-half
(42 percent) thought that television news gave a realistic portrayal of the
amount of violence occurring in society. Of the remaining respondents, 39 percent thought that television overportrayed violence, while 13 percent thought it
underportrayed violence. See Eagleton Poll Archive, Poll 123, question qgv15b,
September 1999, retrieved January 23, 2005 at http://www.scc.rutgers.edu/
eagleton/serverFreq.cfm?quest_Quest_ID_453058 820.

4. News release, Eagleton New Jersey Project, Eagleton Institute of Politics, Rutgers
University, New Brunswick, N.J., September 18, 2002, www.eagleton.rutg-
ers.edu.

5. Harrison A. Williams, foreword to *The Outlook on New Jersey*, edited by Silvio R.
Laccetti (Union City, N.J.: William H. Wise and Co., Inc., 1979), viii.

6. Charles A. Stansfield, Jr., *New Jersey: A Geography* (Boulder, Colo.: Westview
Press, 1983), 3.

7. Joseph A. LeFante, preface to *The Outlook on New Jersey*, edited by Silvio R.
Laccetti (Union City, N.J.: William H. Wise and Co., Inc., 1979), xii.

8. Frank J. Esposito, "New Jersey's Identity Crisis," in *The Outlook on New Jersey*,
edited by Silvio R. Laccetti (Union City, N.J.: William H. Wise and Co., Inc., 1979),
8. Two analysts have suggested that Greater New York's distinct political and
economic state identities have yielded to the homogenizing power of the television broadcast signal. See Gerald Benjamin and Richard P. Nathan, *Regionalism
and Realism: A Study of Governments in the New York Metropolitan Area* (Washington, D.C.: Brookings Institution Press, 2001), 7.

9. U.S. Census Bureau estimates since 2000 have lowered New Jersey's population
ranking to tenth or eleventh nationally. See Robert Gebeloff, "It May Seem
Crowded, but Jersey Growth Lags," *Star-Ledger*, December 22, 2004, 19.

10. Some observers divide New Jersey into three sectors, with Central Jersey lying
between North and South Jersey. Viewers in the center of the state tend to be
oriented variously to the New York or Philadelphia network affiliates.

11. Peggy McGlone, "So Much State Aid, So Few Patrons," *Star-Ledger,* May 1, 2005, 1.

12. Robert Strauss, "New Jersey Public TV, Small but Ambitious," *New York Times,* June 6, 2004, section 14, 1.

13. Although North Jerseyans are more likely to watch New York channels for local news, recent studies suggest that fewer Americans nationally are turning to television for news of any kind. In 2004 a nationwide survey found that a plurality of Americans (42 percent) turn to local television broadcasts for at least some of their news about election campaigns. A smaller but still substantial share (31 percent) relied on daily newspapers. However, compared to an earlier survey in 2000 both media had lost significant audience share owing to the growing popularity of other news sources such as the Internet. See Pew Research Center for the People and the Press, "Cable and Internet Loom Large in Fragmented Political News Universe," news release, retrieved April 2, 2004 at www.pewresearch .org. See also Howard Kurtz, "Survey Says Americans Split on Media Bias," *Star-Ledger,* January 12, 2004, 2

14. Bill Dedman and Stephen K. Doig, "Racial Diversity of the News Staff and Circulation Area Demographics for the *Star-Ledger,* Newark," report of the John S. and James L. Knight Foundation, May 2004, retrieved at http://powerreporting .com/knight/nj_the_star_ledger_newark.html.

15. Pearson Education, publishing as Infoplease, "Top 100 Daily Newspapers in the United States," 2002–4, retrieved at http://www.infoplease.com/ipea/ A0004420. Most of the data are based on partial-week averages. See also Audit Bureau of Circulations, "Top 150 Newspapers by Largest Reported Circulation," October 15, 2004, retrieved at http://www.accessabc.com/reader/top100.htm. These figures tend to be higher because they report the largest circulation, rather than average circulation.

16. Pearson Education, publishing as Infoplease, "Top 100 Daily Newspapers in the United States," 2002–4, retrieved at http://www.infoplease.com/ipea/ A0004420. Unfortunately, precise figures for circulation in North Jersey are unavailable.

17. Dunstan McNichol, "When It Comes to State Politics, Few Are Listening," *Star-Ledger,* June 2, 2003, 9.

18. Jeff, Whelan, "Poll: McGreevey Still Slipping," *Star-Ledger*, September 14, 2003, 1.

19. "The Sorry State of Turnout in New Jersey Elections," *Star-Ledger*/Eagleton-Rutgers Poll, news release 144–7, October 5, 2003, retrieved at http://slerp.rutgers.edu.

20. "Political Knowledge in New Jersey," *Star-Ledger*/Eagleton-Rutgers Poll, news release 143–7, June 1, 2003, retrieved at http://slerp.rutgers.edu.

21. Ibid.

22. From 1995 to 2000 nearly 207,000 people moved from New York State to New Jersey. This was the second largest interstate migration in the United States after that between New York State and Florida. See Marc J. Perry, Table 1: "The 20 Largest State-to-State Migration Flows: 1995–2000," in "State-to-State Migration Flows: 1995 to 2000," *Census 2000 Special Reports* (Washington, D.C.: U.S. Census Bureau, U.S. Department of Commerce, August 2003).

23. In 2000 foreign-born residents comprised 18.5 percent of New Jersey's population, ranking the state third after California and New York. Between 2000 and 2002 an additional 152,000 immigrants moved to New Jersey. See Jonathan Casiano, "Still Flocking to the Land of Opportunity," *Star-Ledger*, November 27, 2002, 2. Among New Jersey's households in 2000, 25.5 percent did not speak English at home. See the Associated Press, "English Is Becoming More Foreign in U.S.," *Star-Ledger*, October 9, 2003, 3. Records show that the heaviest concentration of immigrants is in the six northeastern counties located nearest New York City. See Robert Gebeloff, "Immigrants Keep N.J. Population Growing," *Star-Ledger*, April 17, 2003, 19.

24. From 1995 to 2000 nearly 119,000 people moved from New Jersey to Florida. Among all states sending migrants to Florida, only the flow from New York State was higher. See Perry, "State-to-State Migration Flows," Table 1.

25. A poll in 2003 of New Jerseyans statewide found that 54 percent received most of their New Jersey news from newspapers, while 31 percent did so primarily from television. About 10 percent turned to radio or the Internet. See Eagleton Poll Archive, Poll 143c, question qin3, May 2003, retrieved January 23, 2005 at http://www.scc.rutgers.edu/eagleton/serverFreq.cfm?quest_Quest_ID_453076 160.

26. Thomas F. Coon, "New York City's Giant Shadow," ReaderForum, *Star-Ledger*, January 18, 2002, 20.

27. Ibid.

28. There are also several minor league teams in New Jersey. Including the Newark Bears, there are seven Triple A league baseball teams. The Juggernaut, a professional lacrosse team, as well as three semiprofessional women's soccer clubs, further enrich the sports setting in the state. See Colin Stephenson, "Garden State Growing Sports, Too," *Star-Ledger,* June 18, 2004, 53.

29. Alex Williams, "Back to the Future," *New Yorker* (October 27, 2003), retrieved January 14, 2005 at http://www.newyorkmetro.com/newyorkmetro/news/sports/features/n_9393/. See also Charles V. Bagli, "Deal Is Signed for Nets Arena in Brooklyn," *New York Times,* March 4, 2005, B3.

30. Richard Lezin Jones, "Cheering the Nets, but Without Blushing," *New York Times,* June 9, 2002, 39.

31. The NY/NJ MetroStars, a professional soccer team, plays home games at the Meadowlands Sports Complex and attracts visitors from New York and New Jersey. Fans are drawn heavily from immigrant communities, but soccer in the state is still overshadowed by traditional American sports such as baseball, football, hockey, and basketball.

32. Iver Peterson, "Teams May Be Great, but New Jersey Can't Win," *Star-Ledger,* June 1, 2003, 37.

33. Ibid. See also Jones, 39.

34. Frederick Reicken, "Rooting for East Rutherford," *New York Times,* June 8, 2002, A15.

35. Ibid.

36. John McLaughlin, "Inferior Image, Superior Teams," *Star-Ledger,* June 15, 2003, 21. See also Nick Paumgarten, "Department of Sport—From Jersey," *New Yorker,* June 9, 2003, 18–19.

37. Ronald Smothers, "Party for Devils? More Confetti, Less Asphalt, Fans Say," *New York Times,* June 11, 2002, 1.

38. Some scholars offer empirical support for central city sports venues. See Arthur C. Nelson, "Prosperity or Blight: A Question of Major League Stadia Locations," *Economic Development Quarterly* 15, no. 3 (2001): 255–65.

39. "Newark City, Data for the City in 1980, 1990, and 2000," from "Metropolitan Racial and Ethnic Change—Census 2000," Lewis Mumford Center, State Univer-

sity of New York at Albany, retrieved at http://mumford.albany.edu/census/wholePop/CitySegData.

40. A recent study found that Newark had the fourth highest hardship index among U.S. cities in 2000. The index included measures of unemployment, education, income, poverty, dependency, and housing crowdedness. See Lisa M. Montiel, Richard P. Nathan, and David J. Wright, "Table 1: Cities with Highest Hardship in 2000," in "An Update on Urban Hardship," The Nelson A. Rockefeller Institute of Government, State University of New York at Albany, 2004, 4. For hindsight on Newark's plight, see Kenneth T. Jackson and Barbara B. Jackson, "The Black Experience in Newark—The Growth of the Ghetto, 1870–1970," in *New Jersey Since 1860: New Findings and Interpretations,* edited by William C. Wright (Trenton: New Jersey Historical Commission, 1972), 36–59. See also Clement A. Price, "The Afro-American Community of Newark, 1917–1947: A Social History" (diss., Rutgers University, 1975).

41. U.S. Census Bureau. 2003. Table HS-7, "Population of the Largest 75 Cities: 1900 to 2000," *Statistical Abstract of the United States* (2003): 13–14, retrieved from www.census.gov/statab/hist/HS-07.pdf.

42. Steve Chambers, and Robert Gebeloff, "A Suburban Crossroads Becomes Boom Town," *Star-Ledger,* December 31, 2003, 1, 6.

43. Jonathan Schuppe, "Shots That Echo Forever, *Star-Ledger,* May 15, 2005, 1.

44. For a historical perspective on urban revitalization nationally, see Jon C. Teaford, *The Rough Road to Renaissance: Urban Revitalization in America, 1940–1985* (Baltimore: Johns Hopkins University Press, 1990).

45. Besides its new performing arts center, Newark's cultural legacy includes the Newark Museum, the New Jersey Historical Society, the Newark Public Library, and Newark Symphony Hall. Institutions of higher education include architecture, business, engineering, medical, and dental schools, two law schools, and the Newark campus of Rutgers University. Two civic organizations have substantially improved the city's Branch Brook and Weequahic parks, designed by the firm of Frederick Law Olmsted. The Catholic diocese and other entities have funded a network of community-based organizations that have built affordable housing, shopping facilities, and job training centers.

46. The author was an invited attendee at the October 19, 2000 event. The account is taken from his personal notes.

47. Among the speakers were the minority leader of the state senate, the president of a major local corporation, a leading developer, the head of the state's black clergy organization, the leaders of two local foundations, and the president of the YankeeNets organization, co-owners of the Nets at that time.

48. Ronald Smothers, "Treffinger Pleads Guilty to Corruption," *New York Times*, May 31, 2003, B1.

49. In particular, the *Star-Ledger*'s Matthew Futterman, Jeffrey Mays and George Jordan have stood out for their investigative work on the arena proposal.

50. Matthew Futterman, "Winning Isn't Everything," *Star-Ledger,* May 16, 2003, 63.

51. See, for example, Costas Spiroli and Larry Bennett, *It's Hardly Sportin': Stadiums, Neighborhoods, and the New Chicago* (Dekalb, Ill.: Northern Illinois University Press, 2003); Roger G. Noll and Andrew Zimbalist, eds., *Sports, Jobs, and Taxes: The Economic Impacts of Sports Teams and Stadiums* (Washington, D.C.: Brookings Institution, 1997); Marc Rosentraub, *Major League Losers: The Real Costs of Sports and Who's Paying for It* (New York: Basic Books, 1997); and Charles C. Euchner, *Playing the Field: Why Sports Teams Move and Cities Fight to Keep Them* (Baltimore: Johns Hopkins University Press, 1993).

52. "The Newark Nets—A Tough Sell," *Star-Ledger*/Eagleton-Rutgers Poll, news release SL/ER 71–2 (EP121–2), January 26, 1999, retrieved at http://slerp .rutgers.edu/retrieve. The survey also found that 29 percent of the respondents were less likely to attend a Nets game in Newark than at the Meadowlands arena and only 7 percent were more likely. In addition, there were racial disparities in support, with blacks much more interested in attending a Newark game than whites. Among people with less interest in attending games in Newark, most were wary about safety, inconvenience, or parking problems, or said that the city was a less attractive place than the Meadowlands arena.

53. "Sports Star Wars: Where to Build the New Arena(s)," *Star-Ledger*/Eagleton-Rutgers Poll, news release SL/EP 72–3 (EP122–3), May 23, 1999, retrieved at http://slerp.rutgers.edu/retrieve.

54. Dennis Gale, Wayne Eastman, and Robert T. Guerette, "Tourist Bubbles, Con-

sumption Districts, and Suburban Visitors to the City: When Small May Be Beautiful" (unpublished paper presented at the annual meeting of the Urban Affairs Association in Cleveland, Ohio, March 27–30, 2003).

55. John Brennan, "Little Backing for New Arena," *The Record,* May 5, 2002, 1.

56. "Newark Arena Makes No Progress with Public," PublicMind, Fairleigh Dickinson University, 2002, retrieved May 29, 2003 at http://publicmind.fdu.edu/arena2/. Twenty-two percent of the respondents said they would be more likely to attend an event at a Newark arena than at the Meadowlands, while 50 percent would be less likely to do so. Blacks were about three times more likely to attend a Newark event than whites. A similar survey in 2003 found that opinions had changed little over the preceding year.

57. Jeff Whelan, "The Crowd Yawns Over Fate of Nets," *Star-Ledger,* September 10, 2003, 1. Most respondents either did not feel strongly about professional sports or did not feel that public subsidies are an appropriate way to keep the teams in-state. Moreover, not only was support weak for a Newark arena, sharp racial disparities revealed considerably more support from blacks than from whites.

58. One factor influencing the governor was opposition to a Newark arena from influential politicians in Bergen County, where the Meadowlands complex is located.

59. The Port Authority of New York and New Jersey agreed to pay Newark $265 million for rental increases on the city-owned Newark Liberty International Airport (which the Authority operates).

60. Jeffrey C. Mays, "City Residents File Suit to Block Arena Deal," *Star-Ledger,* November 22, 2002, 35.

61. Ibid. Mayor James's response reminded some Jerseyans of Frank Hague, the late Jersey City machine boss who claimed, "I am the law." See Dayton D. McKean, *The Boss: The Hague Machine in Action* (Boston: Houghton Mifflin Co., 1940), 224, 270–71.

62. A measure of the controversy over the arena proposal is revealed in newspaper op-ed pages. One writer charged that the mayor had "suckered the city council" and "hoodwinked" the public and that the plan was "foolishness," "stupidity," and "criminal behavior." Another critic noted the irony of spending the money on an arena while neglecting public education so that Newark youngsters can

"sell hot dogs and remove cigarette butts from urinals" instead of "getting an education that will serve them in the future." Some writers, however, have endorsed the arena. See "Debate on the Newark Arena Deal," ReaderForum, respectively, letters from James R. Heckel (Sparta) and Patricia Weston Rivera (Newark), *Star-Ledger*, October 24, 2002, 16.

63. Joshua Robin. "MTA Approves Nets Arena," *Newsday*, September 15, 2005, 1, retrieved at http://www.newsday.com/sports/basketball/nets.

64. Matthew Futterman and Jeff Mays, "Mayor Rolls Out Red (and Black) Carpet for Devils," *Star-Ledger*, February 13, 2004, 23.

65. Matthew Futterman, "Sports Authority: Dueling Arenas Are Just Fine with Us," *Star-Ledger*, February 19, 2004, 17.

66. Jonathan D. Glater, "NHL's Financial Analysis Reveals Significant Losses," *New York Times*, February 13, 2004, 1, retrieved from www.nytimes.com/2003/02/13/sports/hockey/13FINA.html. Nineteen NHL team franchises averaged $18 million each in operating losses while eleven others posted average profits of $6.4 million. The study reported that the NHL was "on a treadmill to obscurity."

67. Futterman and Mays, 23.

68. William Kleinknecht, "Clash of New York Titans Holds Key to Jets' Future," *Star-Ledger*, October 3, 2004, section 1, 29; Laura Mansnerus, "New Meadowlands Stadium Is Approved for the Giants," *New York Times*, April 23, 2005, B6; Charles V. Bagli, "Jets and Giants Hail Arena Plan, and Codey," *New York Times*, December 13, 2005, B5.

69. Michael N. Danielson and Jameson W. Doig, *New York: The Politics of Urban Regional Development* (Berkeley and Los Angeles: University of California Press, 1982), 148–49.

Chapter 5

1. Critics of North Jersey's image sometimes point to the seemingly unrelieved panorama of truck stops, diners, filling stations, fast-food franchises, sprawling shopping malls, corporate parks, and national chain stores. Travelers along the Garden State Parkway, for example, plunge through a linear landscape of faded apartment buildings, withering frame houses, and gritty commercial districts in Irvington, East Orange, and Orange. A sprawling cemetery's closely packed

headstones mimic in death the crowded tenor of life for many people in these communities. Indeed, as Tony Soprano's car emerges from the Lincoln Tunnel in the opening scenes of television's *The Sopranos,* images of the seedy landscapes near Jersey City and Newark portray the worst of North Jersey stereotypes. Yet, these depictions are selective and miss the many attractive and scenic features not visible from key highways.

2. See, for example, Michael Aaron Rockland, "Image," in *New Jersey Encyclopedia,* edited by Maxine N. Lurie and Marc Mappen (New Brunswick, N.J.: Rutgers University Press, 2004), 401–2; and Debra Galant, "What Reputation?" *New York Times,* October 6, 2002, section 14, 1,.

3. Mark Stuart, *Gangster No. 2: Longy Zwillman, the Man Who Invented Organized Crime* (Secaucus, N.J.: Lyle Stuart). See also Marc Mappen, *Jerseyana: The Underside of New Jersey History* (New Brunswick, N.J.: Rutgers University Press, 1992), 214–17.

4. Richard Hammer, *Playboy's Illustrated History of Organized Crime* (Chicago: Playboy Press, 1973), 93–95.

5. Stuart, 75–77; and Hank Messick and Burt Goldblatt, *The Mobs and the Mafia* (New York: Thomas Y. Crowell Co., 1973), 105–6. Messick and Goldblatt, among others, indicate that at first the commission was termed the Big Seven.

6. Although Longy Zwillman was well respected by his New York partners, they did not hesitate to employ violence in North Jersey to achieve their ends. In the fall of 1935 the infamous Dutch Schultz (aka Arthur Flegenheimer) was gunned down in Newark's Palace Chop House by gangsters believed to be employed by the syndicate leadership in New York. See Mappen, 198–200.

7. Senator Carey Estes Kefauver (D-Tenn.) chaired hearings of the Special Committee on Organized Crime in Interstate Commerce, commonly termed the Kefauver Committee. Held in fourteen cities, with eight hundred witnesses, the sessions drew the attention of millions of Americans. Because several of the key organized crime figures were from New York and New Jersey, much negative publicity resulted.

8. Hammer, 256–59; and Jay Robert Nash, *Bloodletters and Badmen* (New York: M. Evans and Co., Inc., 1973), 15–16, 21–22, 626. Several mobsters with New York connections were active in North Jersey. Willie Moretti, a Mafia captain with

extensive racketeering enterprises in North Jersey, was executed in a Cliffside Park, New Jersey restaurant in 1951 on orders of Vito Genovese, a New York Mafia member. Joe Adonis, a Mafia board member, ran his New Jersey rackets from another Cliffside Park restaurant and fled to Italy in 1953 under threat of tax evasion charges and a conviction for violation of immigration laws. And an underworld executioner and board member, Albert Anastasia, who lived in Fort Lee, New Jersey, was gunned down in Manhattan in 1957, also on orders of Genovese. All three men had extensive ties to the Mafia going back to the early 1930s.

9. Retrieved on February 1, 2004 from the New Jersey Commission of Investigation website: http://www.state.nj.us/sci/overviewoc.htm. Though several of these men were convicted on income tax evasion or contempt of court charges, most were associated with crimes such as bookmaking, numbers operation, gambling, loan-sharking, bribery, and even murder. Most of these gangsters were subsequently murdered or died of natural causes.

10. Robert Rudolph, *The Boys from New Jersey* (New York: William Morrow and Co., Inc., 1992), 18.

11. Ibid., 19.

12. Ibid., 81–82.

13. Robert Rudolph and Guy Sterling, "Jersey Mob Soon to Get Infusion of Old Blood," *Star-Ledger,* April 10, 2002, 1.

14. Robert Rudolph and Tom Hester, "Mob Ring Broken Up, Police Say," *Star-Ledger,* June 11, 2003, 13.

15. "Federal Judge Appoints Monitor to Reform Mob-Tainted Hotel and Restaurant Union," news release, U.S. Attorney's Office, Newark, N.J., April 17, 2002.

16. Donald W. Cox, *Mafia Wipeout: How the Feds Put Away an Entire Mob Family* (New York: Shapolsky Publishers, Inc., 1989); and Joseph Salerno and Stephen J. Rivele, *The Plumber: The True Story of How One Good Man Helped Destroy the Entire Philadelphia Mafia* (New York: Knightsbridge Publishing Co., 1990).

17. George Freselone and Robert J. Wagman, *Blood Oath* (New York: Simon and Schuster, 1994).

18. "Nicodemo Scarfo Pleads Guilty to Running New Jersey Gambling Ring," news release, U.S. Attorney's Office, Newark, N.J., February 2, 2002.

19. Guy Sterling, "Mob Boss Louis Gatto Dies in Prison Hospital," *Star-Ledger,* Sep-

tember 10, 2002, 31. Gatto was closely associated with Vincent "The Chin" Gigante and Anthony "Fat Tony" Salerno, then the boss and the underboss, respectively, of the Genovese crime family. Two of Gatto's sons were also imprisoned.

20. "Notorious Mafia Leader 'Joe Bananas' Dies at 97," *Star-Ledger,* May 12, 2002, 24; and Alan Feuer, "Gotti's Funeral Procession Takes in His Old Haunts," *New York Times,* June 16, 2002, 27.

21. Larry McShane, "It's a First: 5 Mob Bosses in Prison Simultaneously," *Star-Ledger,* February 2, 2003, 36. See also William Glaberson, "Old Mobs Never Die, and Cliched but Brutal Methods Refuse to Fade Away," *New York Times,* January 26, 2003, 27.

22. Rudolph Sterling, 1.

23. Robert Schwaneberg, "Mafia Remains a Force to Be Reckoned With," *Star-Ledger,* May 1, 2003, 25.

24. Clark R. Mollenhoff, *Strike Force: Organized Crime and the Government* (Englewood Cliffs, N.J.: Prentice-Hall, Inc., 1972), 8–9.

25. Carl Sifakis, "The DeCavalcante Tapes: FBI Eavesdropping," in *The Mafia Encyclopedia,* 2d ed. (New York: Facts on File, 1999), 110–11.

26. "Acting Boss of DeCavalcante Crime Family and Four Others Indicted for Racketeering," news release, U.S. Attorney's Office, Newark, N.J., April 10, 2001. See also Jonathan Kwitny, *Vicious Circles: The Mafia in the Marketplace* (New York: W. W. Norton and Co., 1979), 57.

27. Robert Rudolph, "How a Crime Family Turned Dysfunctional," *Star-Ledger,* May 9, 2003, 1. Rudolph quotes Kevin McCarthy, the former head of the U.S. Attorney's Organized Crime Strike Force, who made the comments. McCarthy's staff investigated the DeCavalcante family for years.

28. Ibid. See also Robert Rudolph, "Tales Point to Bumbling Mobsters," *Star-Ledger,* May 16, 2003, 17.

29. Ibid. See also Robert Rudolph, "Jersey Mafia Boss Admits Ordering Hit," *Star-Ledger,* September 5, 2003, 20.

30. One study of the DeCavalcante family states that they were "openly called 'farmers' by the New York goodfella crowd," a measure of obvious disrespect coming from the capital of organized crime in America. See Greg B. Smith, *Made Men* (New York: Berkley Books, 2003), 14.

31. Author's interview with Kevin McCarthy, the former head of the federal Organized Crime Task Force, Newark, N.J., January 14, 2004.

32. The first recorded bribe of a public official in New Jersey may have occurred in 1703, when Lord Cornbury, a provincial governor, accepted money from landowners seeking advantage in upcoming elections for the provincial Assembly. See Marc Mappen, 16–19.

33. But the state's admirable record in national politics has been tainted in recent times. The 1980 conviction of U.S. Senator Harrison Williams in the congressional Abscam scandal and the more recent admonishment of U.S. Senator Robert Torricelli in 2002 by the Senate ethics committee (followed by his resignation from the Senate) shocked voters in New Jersey. Torricelli admitted to having received a television and a CD player, which he partially paid for, as well as jewelry, from a political friend.

34. Ronald Smothers, "Treffinger Pleads Guilty to Corruption," *New York Times,* May 31, 2003, B1. Treffinger acknowledged that he applied for the job of U.S. Attorney under the administration of President George W. Bush in the hopes that this authority would help him eliminate the investigation then plaguing him.

35. Diane C. Walsh, "Ex-Essex Exec Paid Himself $65,000," *Star-Ledger,* August 18 2002, 22.

36. William Kleinknecht, "Gibson Gets Probation in Plea Bargain," *Star-Ledger,* November 1, 2002, 1. Gibson, celebrated in the 1970s as one of the first black mayors of a major American city, left office in 1986.

37. Addonizio was once quoted, "You don't make much money as a congressman, but as mayor you can make a million bucks." See John Farmer, Jr., "Culture of Corruption," *Star-Ledger,* April 28, 2002, 1.

38. Kevin C. Dilworth, "Bost Admits Witness Tampering, Ends Trial," *Star-Ledger,* April 24, 2003, 13; and John P. Martin and Kevin C. Dilworth, "Former Irvington Mayor Gets Jail," *Star-Ledger,* September 9, 2003, 19. Bost is a former Essex County freeholder (that is, an elected member of the county's legislative council) and served as mayor of Irvington for eight years.

39. Martin and Dilworth. 19.

40. Ana M. Alaya, "Paterson Mayor Admits to Fraud," *Star-Ledger,* July 2, 2002, 13; and John P. Martin, "Ex-Paterson Mayor Gets 37-Month Term," *Star-Ledger,* April 28, 2003, 15.

41. "Former Paterson City Public Works Director Pleads Guilty to Accepting Cash from Vendor," news release, U.S. Attorney's Office, Newark, New Jersey, July 15, 2002.

42. "Former Passaic County Administrator DiDonna Sentenced to Four Months in Prison," news release, U.S. Attorney's Office, Newark, N.J., October 31, 2001. Murphy, who had served about one year of a 43-month sentence, was released in 2002 after an appeals court ordered a new trial.

43. Josh Margolin, "Feds Will Monitor Elections in Passaic," *Star-Ledger,* November 1, 2003, 12.

44. "'Quality of Government' Ratings Decline Steeply in New Jersey," news release, Eagleton Institute of Politics, Rutgers University, New Brunswick, N.J., March 2, 2003, retrieved at http://slerp.rutgers.edu/retrieve.

45. Jonathan Schuppe, "Jerseyans: Politicians and Graft Go Together," *Star-Ledger,* June 26, 2002, 13.

46. Ibid.

47. Jeffrey C. Mays, "Councilman Ends 28-Year Stint," *Star-Ledger,* June 28, 2002, 37–38.

48. John Farmer, Jr., "Culture of Corruption," *Star-Ledger,* April 28, 2002, section 10, 1.

49. "Rejoining the Fight on Official Corruption," editorial, *Star-Ledger,* November 12, 2002, 10.

50. Laura Mansnerus, "Old-Fashioned Graft," *New York Times,* October 30, 2002, A1.

51. Laura Mansnerus, "New Jersey Struggles to Change Its Campaign Finance Laws," *New York Times,* May 21, 2004, B4.

52. Josh Getlin, "Locking Up N.J.'s Bad Guys," *Los Angeles Times,* February 27, 2003, A1.

53. Michael Barone, Grant Ujifusa, and Douglas Matthews, *The Almanac of American Politics, 1974* (Boston: Gambit, 1973), 602. A later edition of the almanac declared that "New Jersey, once corrupt, is now pretty well cleaned up." Michael Barone and Grant Ujifusa, *The Almanac of American Politics, 1992* (Washington, D.C.: National Journal, 1991), 771.

54. "An Honest Man in New Jersey?" *The Economist,* May 8, 2003, retrieved July 12, 2004 at www.economist.com/PrinterFriendly.cfm?Story_ID = 17774688.

55. Tom Hester, "Nader Lists Beefs with D.C. and Trenton," *Star-Ledger,* September 1, 2004, 19.

56. Observers have long pondered whether political crimes are more common in North Jersey and statewide than in other states. There is little evidence to clarify the issue. But one study examined U.S. Department of Justice data and found that in 2002 New Jersey ranked sixteenth among the fifty states in the percentage of federal corruption convictions per one hundred thousand state residents. Ranking first, second, and third were Mississippi, North Dakota, and Louisiana, respectively. New York, the only eastern state in the top ten, ranked tenth. See "Public Corruption in the United States," a report released at the National Press Club, Washington, D.C. by the Corporate Crime Reporter, January 16, 2004.

57. Between 1966 and 1990 Hoboken lost nearly half of its employment. The most severe declines occurred in manufacturing employment, where the number of jobs decreased from 15,600 in 1966 to 4,200 in 1990. But these losses were partially offset by increases in service employment, from almost 1,300 jobs in 1966 to more than 4,300 in 1990.

58. Steve Chambers and Robert Gebeloff, "A Suburban Crossroads Becomes Boom Town," *Star-Ledger,* December 31, 2003, 1, 6.

59. Census 2000, *American FactFinder*, Jersey City and Hoboken, N.J. files, Summary File 1 (SF 1) and Summary File 3 (SF 3) (Washington, D.C.: Bureau of the Census), retrieved December 14, 2005 at http://factfinder.census.gov.

60. A regional study of employment commuting in 1997–98 discovered that 29 percent of work trips originating in Hudson County were destined for Manhattan. This percentage was much higher than that of any other New Jersey county. A sampling error of at least +/- 5 percent is indicated. See "Travel in the New York-New Jersey Metropolitan Area, Appendix: County Data for Maps," New York Metropolitan Transportation Council and New Jersey Transportation Planning Authority, April 2000, 14.

61. Helene Stapinski's memoir of growing up in Jersey City in the 1970s and 1980s is especially revealing. She describes endemic dishonesty on the streets and in government at a time just preceding the city's remarkable social and physical transformation. See Helene Stapinski, *Five-Fingered Discount: A Crooked Family History* (New York: Random House, 2002).

62. Melvin G. Holli, *The American Mayor: The Best and the Worst Big-City Leaders* (University Park: Pennsylvania State University Press, 1999), 12–13.

63. Ibid., 13.

64. Richard J. Connors, *A Cycle of Power: The Career of Jersey City Mayor Frank Hague* (Metuchen, N.J.: The Scarecrow Press, Inc., 1971), 76–80. For additional insights see Dayton McKean, *The Boss: The Hague Machine in Action* (Boston: Houghton-Mifflin, 1940).

65. Stapinski, 70.

66. Connors, 72–75.

67. Ibid., 145–46.

68. For a somewhat more sympathetic accounting of Hague's record, see Alan J. Karcher, *New Jersey's Multiple Municipal Madness* (New Brunswick, N.J.: Rutgers University Press, 1999), 183–86.

69. Stapinski, 201–4.

70. "Former Hoboken Mayor Russo Indicted for Extortion and Bribery," news release, U.S. Attorney's Office, Newark, N.J., September 25, 2003. See also Ronald Smothers, "Ex-Mayor of Hoboken Admits He Accepted $5000 in Bribes," *New York Times,* September 30, 2004, B6.

71. Robert Rudolph, "Ex-Official in N. Bergen Gets 3 Years for Mail Fraud," *Star-Ledger,* July 12, 2003, 4. See also Guy Sterling, "Third N. Bergen Official Admits Graft in Continuing U.S. Probe," *Star-Ledger,* July 18, 2002, 22; and Robert Rudolph, "Third Official Admits Guilt in Hudson Corruption Probe," *Star-Ledger,* September 21, 2002, 26.

72. John P. Martin and Robert Rudolph, "Fallen Power Broker's Plea: Guilty," *Star-Ledger,* October 4, 2002, 1.

73. John P. Martin, "Freeholder in Hudson Took Bribes," *Star-Ledger,* June 30, 2004, 15.

74. John P. Martin, "Ex-Hudson Freeholder Gets 37 Months for Graft," *Star-Ledger,* December 16, 2003, 21; and John P. Martin, "Hudson Official Indicted in State Corruption Probe," *Star-Ledger,* October 30, 2002, 13.

75. Rudy Larini, "Accountant Paid Bribes for Hudson Contracts," *Star-Ledger,* July 26, 2003, 4. See also John P. Martin, "Pal Admits Passing Bribes to Janiszewski,"

Star-Ledger, July 20, 2004, 1; and John P. Martin, "Judge Jails Builder with Midas Touch," *Star-Ledger,* October 22, 2004, 1.

76. "Lawmen Seek Takeover of Longshoremen's Union," *Star-Ledger,* December 11, 2002, 10; and Larry McShane, "Saga of Crime Is an Old Story on the Waterfront," *Star-Ledger,* 37. By early 2004, one ex-president of Local 1588 had been indicted and his two predecessors had pleaded guilty to conspiring to embezzle funds from the union.

77. Ronald Leir, "Former ILA Prez Won't Do Time," *Jersey Journal,* November 20, 2004, 1.

78. McShane, 37, 41.

79. "Former Jersey City Man Convicted of Racketeering, Multiple Murders," news release of the U.S. Attorney's Office, Newark, N.J., July 11, 2002.

80. "Bonnano Crime Family Member and His Associate Sentenced to Prison for Conspiracy to Commit Extortion," news release, U.S. Attorney's Office, Newark, N.J., June 24, 2003. Taglianetti and Pastore were from New York's Staten Island, which is connected to North Jersey by bridges. Both men were identified as members of the Bonnano crime family.

Chapter 6

1. David W. Chen, "Suburbs to City: Drop the Attitude," *New York Times,* November 24, 2002, B33.

2. Ibid. Author Chen quotes economists Mark Goloven and Thomas J. Spitznas, respectively.

3. One study included some of the counties in Outer North Jersey in a subregion it termed the "Wealth Belt." See James W. Hughes, Joseph J. Seneca, and Connie O. Hughes, "Anticipating Census 2000: New Jersey's Emerging Demographic Profile," *Rutgers Regional Report* (Edward J. Bloustein School of Planning and Public Policy, Rutgers University), issue paper no. 18 (July 2000): 9–13.

4. "A Quarter Century of New Jersey Developments: Successes and Failures," *Star-Ledger*/Eagleton-Rutgers Poll, news release SL/EP 74–2 (EP124–2), December 19, 1999, retrieved at http://slerp.rutgers.edu/retrieve.

5. "New Jersey and Rodney Dangerfield: Perfect Together," The *Star-Ledger*/Eagle-

ton-Rutgers Poll, news release 143–4, May 18, 2003, retrieved at http://
slerp.rutgers.edu/retrieve.

6. Ibid.

7. "New Jerseyans: Love the State, Hate the Taxes, and Don't Care What Other Americans Think," Fairleigh Dickinson University. PublicMind Poll, Tables 2–7, August 2, 2001, retrieved August 4, 2001 from http://publicmind.fdu.edu/ sameorbetter.index.html.

8. "New Jersey and Rodney Dangerfield: Perfect Together," *Star-Ledger*/Eagleton-Rutgers Poll, news release 143–4, May 18, 2003, retrieved at http://slerp .rutgers.edu/retrieve.

9. For example, the largest source of nonimmigrant movers to New Jersey is New York State, from which nearly 207,000 people relocated between 1995 and 2000. See Marc J. Perry, Table 2: "Largest Migration Inflow and Outflow by State: 1995 to 2000," in "State-to-State Migration Flows: 1995 to 2000," *Census 2000 Special Reports* (Washington, D.C.: U.S. Census Bureau, U.S. Department of Commerce, August 2003), retrieved December 4, 2004 at http://www.census.gov/ prod/2003pubs/censr-8.pdf.

10. Corey Kilgannon, "City Limits," *New York Times,* April 28, 2002, section 14, 1.

11. Staten Island, the fifth borough of New York City, has largely escaped the attention of humorists, it seems. Its higher socioeconomic profile and more suburban character may account for this.

12. *Sleeper,* written and directed by Woody Allen, MGM/United Artists Studios, 1973.

13. Calvin Trillin, *Tepper Isn't Going Out* (New York: Random House, 2001), 6.

14. Dave Barry, "Pentagon Preparing for Era of Stench Warfare," *Star-Ledger,* April 7, 2002, section 10, 6.

15. Russell Baker, *Growing Up* (New York: New American Library, 1982), 124.

16. For a like-minded viewpoint, see Stephen Whitty, "Change Always a Part of the City," *Sunday Star-Ledger,* November 11, 2001, section 4, 5.

17. Most of these people are listed in "Made in New Jersey" retrieved at http:// www.state.nj.us/travel/facts&fun/madeinnj.html, April 22, 2005.

18. From "Singin' Jersey," retrieved at http://www.nj.com/springsteen, April 10, 2005.

19. Ibid.

20. Ibid.

FURTHER READING

Adams, Thomas. 1931. *Regional Plan of New York and Its Environs.* Vol. 2, *The Building of the City.* Philadelphia: William F. Fell Co. Reprint, New York: Arno Press, 1974.

Bebout, John E., and Ronald J. Grele. 1964. *Where Cities Meet: The Urbanization of New Jersey.* Vol. 22. The New Jersey Historical Series. Princeton, N.J.: D. Van Nostrand Co., Inc.

Benjamin, Gerald, and Richard P. Nathan. 2001. *Regionalism and Realism: A Study of Governments in the New York Metropolitan Area.* Washington, D.C.: Brookings Institution Press.

Cohen, Lizabeth. 2003. *A Consumer's Republic: The Politics of Mass Consumption in Postwar America.* New York: Alfred A. Knopf.

Connors, Richard J. 1971. *A Cycle of Power: The Career of Jersey City Mayor Frank Hague.* Metuchen, N.J.: Scarecrow Press, Inc.

Cranmer, H. Jerome. 1964. *New Jersey in the Automobile Age: A History of Transportation.* Princeton, N.J.: D. Van Nostrand Co., Inc.

Danielson, Michael N. 1976. *The Politics of Exclusion.* New York: Columbia University Press.

Danielson, Michael N., and Jameson W. Doig. 1982. *New York: The Politics of Urban Regional Development.* Berkeley and Los Angeles: University of California Press.

Doig, Jameson W. 2001. *Empire on the Hudson: Entrepreneurial Vision and Political Power at the Port of New York Authority.* New York: Columbia University Press.

Fleming, Thomas. 1977. *New Jersey: A Bicentennial History.* New York: W. W. Norton and Co., Inc.

Garreau, Joel. 1991. *Edge City: Life on the New Frontier.* New York: Doubleday, Anchor Books.

Gottmann, Jean. 1961. *Megalopolis: The Urbanized Northeastern Seaboard of the United States*. New York: Twentieth Century Fund.

Hoover, Edgar M., and Raymond Vernon. 1959. *Anatomy of a Metropolis: The Changing Distribution of People and Jobs within the New York Metropolitan Region*. Cambridge, Mass.: Harvard University Press.

Kirp, David L., John P. Dwyer, and Larry A. Rosenthal. 1995. *Our Town: Race, Housing, and the Soul of Suburbia*. New Brunswick, N.J.: Rutgers University Press.

Laccetti, Silvio R., ed. 1979. *The Outlook on New Jersey*. Union City, N.J.: William H. Wise and Co., Inc.

Lang, Robert E. 2003. *Edgeless Cities: Exploring the Elusive Metropolis*. Washington, D.C.: Brookings Institution Press.

Lurie, Maxine N., and Marc Mappen, eds. 2004. *The Encyclopedia of New Jersey*. New Brunswick, N.J.: Rutgers University Press.

Mappen, Marc. 1992. *Jerseyana: The Underside of New Jersey History*. New Brunswick, N.J.: Rutgers University Press.

McConville, Brendan. 1999. *Those Daring Disturbers of the Public Peace: The Struggle for Property and Power in Early New Jersey*. Ithaca, N.Y.: Cornell University Press.

McCormick, Richard P. 1981. *New Jersey: From Colony to State*. Revised ed. Newark: New Jersey Historical Society.

Parambo, Ron. 1971. *No Cause for Indictment: An Autopsy of Newark*. New York: Holt, Rinehart, and Winston.

Pomfret, John E. 1973. *Colonial New Jersey: A History*. New York: Charles Scribner's Sons.

Stansfield, Charles A., Jr. 1983. *New Jersey: A Geography*. Boulder, Colo.: Westview Press.

Stapinski, Helene. 2002. *Five-Finger Discount: A Crooked Family History*. New York: Random House.

Stonecash, Jeffrey M., with Mary P. McGuire. 2003. *The Emergence of State Government: Parties and New Jersey Politics, 1950–2000*. Madison and Teaneck, N.J.: Fairleigh Dickinson University Press.

Sullivan, Robert. 1998. *The Meadowlands: Wilderness Adventures on the Edge of a City*. New York: Doubleday, Anchor Books.

Wacker, Peter O. 1975. *Land and People: A Cultural Geography of New Jersey: Origins and Settlement Patterns.* New Brunswick, N.J.: Rutgers University Press.

Weiher, Gregory R. 1991. *The Fractured Metropolis: Political Fragmentation and Metropolitan Segregation.* Albany: State University of New York Press.

Wood, Robert C. 1961. *1400 Governments.* Cambridge, Mass.: Harvard University Press.

Worton, Stanley N., Wilbur E. Apgar, Daniel Jacobson, and Abraham Resnick. 1964. *New Jersey: Past and Present.* New York: Hayden Book Co., Inc.

Yaro, Robert D., and Tony Hiss. 1996. *Region at Risk: The Third Regional Plan for the New York-New Jersey-Connecticut Metropolitan Area.* Regional Plan Association. Washington, D.C. and Covelo, Calif.: Island Press.

INDEX

identity, 79–106, 142–48

image, 107–38, 142–48

immigration, 29, 37–41, 72–77. *See also* Latinos

income, 40, 71

Indianapolis, Ind., 65

Inner North Jersey, 141, 144

Inner Tier Counties, 13. *See also* Inner North Jersey

interracial relationships, 4–6, 42, 44, 47–50, 73, 92–98, 102

interstate highways, 7, 52–53, 77

Irish, 37–38

Irish Americans, 41

Irvington, N.J., 41, 43, 92, 116

Italian Americans, 41

Jackson, N.J., 110

James, Sharpe (mayor), 95, 98–104

Janiszewski, Robert (county executive), 129, 136. *See also* political corruption

Jersey City, N.J., 8, 9, 16, 20–21, 25, 39, 46, 71, 86, 91; case study of, 120–37; crustal urbanization, 64–65; proximity to Manhattan, 28–31; revitalization of, 119–38; water sources of, 61–62; white flight from, 53

Jersey Meadowlands, 7, 9. *See also* Hudson County

Kearny, N.J., 64

labor unions, 110–11, 136–37. *See also* organized crime

land consumption, 56–57, 64–66

Latinos, 40, 44, 72–78, 95

Lenne Lenapi Indians, 36–37

Lincoln Tunnel, 15, 22–23, 108

local affiliate television broadcasting, 79–83

local government, 68–69

localism, 56–57, 62–69, 139, 141–42

Long Island, N.Y., 15, 30, 114

Los Angeles, Calif., 17, 65, 114

Los Angeles Times, 119

Louisville, Ky., 65

Lower East Side, 15, 16

Luciano, Charles "Lucky," 108. *See also* organized crime

Madison, N.J., 1, 70

Madison Square Garden, 15, 88–89

Mafia, 108, 112–13. *See also* organized crime

Manhattan, 3, 7, 8, 11, 13, 15, 16, 18, 43, 51; bi-state conflict, 30–31, 33–34; mass media, 80; North Jersey identity, 140, 142–43, 145; North Jersey relationships, 20–24, 27; organized crime, 108, 114; sports teams, 87, 89; suburbanites' ties to, 36, 46, 53, 55, 71, 77–78, 120, 122. *See also* Gotham; New York City

Manhattan-North Jersey, axis, 13–14, 19, 33, 78, 105, 139; landscape, 1–10; transit, 23

Maplewood, N.J., 3–4, 16, 41, 50

mass media, 79–88, 91, 138

McCann, Gerald (mayor), 129. *See also* political corruption

McCormick, Richard P., 37–38

McGreevy, James (governor), 54

megalopolis, 16–17

Mendham, N.J., 70

Methodists, 38

Metropolitan Regional Council, 28